From the Silence of the Stacks,

New
Voices
Rise

An anthology of writing by The London Library Emerging Writers Programme 2023-24 Cohort

*

Edited by Claire Berliner

Published 2024 by The London Library

The London Library
14 St James's Square, London SW1Y 4LG
londonlibrary.co.uk
Charity No. 312175

ISBN (print) 978-0-9553277-9-7
ISBN (ebook) 978-1-0685123-0-8

Typeset by Will Dady, 2024
Design by Matt Bourne of Level Partnership Ltd

Printed and bound in Great Britain by Clays Ltd, Elcograf S.p.A.

Contents

Stage & Screen

About The London Library

F ounded in 1841, The London Library is one of the world's great lending libraries. A unique literary oasis in the heart of London, it houses an extraordinary collection of around one million books and periodicals dating from 1700 to the present day, nearly all of which can be borrowed.

Members can browse 17 miles of atmospheric bookstacks, read and write in hidden corners or in beautiful reading rooms, attend our vibrant events programme or work remotely using the extensive online resources.

From the outset, the Library has been a place of inspiration and support to writers, readers and thinkers of all kinds. From Charles Dickens to Sarah Waters, T S Eliot to Raymond Antrobus, Virginia Woolf to Kazuo Ishiguro, Angela Carter to Jessie Burton and to successive cohorts participating in our thriving Emerging Writers Programme, our building in St James's Square has provided a home and a creative community for anyone who loves the written word.

The London Library
Emerging Writers Programme

T he London Library Emerging Writers Programme has been running since 2019 for up to 40 participants each year. It is a year-long programme designed to provide early-career writers with the support, resources and community that they need to establish themselves and hone their craft.

The Programme includes: a year's free membership of the Library, with full access to all its resources; a structured programme of masterclasses with established writers and industry professionals; peer support meetings and a writing network; and support from the Library's expert staff. Writers of any genre, age, level of writing experience and from anywhere in the country, are welcome to apply – for free – for a place on the Programme. The only criteria are that applicants have to have a project in mind to work on throughout the year, they have to commit to using the space and collection of the Library and they must not have previously had a full work published or produced. Applications are judged anonymously by a panel of judges drawn from across the literary world.

Previous participants on the Programme have gone on to find agents, publishers and multiple platforms for their work. Some have enjoyed international success and many have found critical acclaim. A number of the communities and networks created on the programme have been sustained long after the year's end and participants have gone on to contribute to future iterations of the Programme.

Introduction

W hen Virginia Woolf, a life member of The London Library, wrote *A Room of One's Own*, she pinpointed what it is that a person needs if they want to become a writer: space (a room), of course, but also time; access to the tools and materials one needs to research, learn and hone ideas; acceptance into a community of writers and thinkers; recognition, validation, belief in one's own right to write. Woolf would, herself, have found those conditions in The London Library, an institution founded in 1841 – and continuing today – to be an inclusive and conducive environment in which to nurture creativity and acquire knowledge. The Emerging Writers Programme began in 2019 with the same intention, to open the space widely and warmly, to recognise talent and incubate it, develop it and send it out into the world. Successive cohorts of the Programme have embarked on the shared endeavour to explore, create, learn, be inspired and to develop both their work and themselves as writers. They have supported each other, built communities, sustained friendships and produced countless works which are now on the Library's shelves and on shelves all over the world.

The application process for this Programme gets increasingly competitive each year and the fifth cohort, whose work is collected in this anthology, were selected from almost 1400 applications. They used their place on the Programme to work on projects that spanned fiction, poetry, memoir, narrative non-fiction, writing for the stage and the screen and, for the first time, translation. The projects are fascinating, revelatory, funny and profound, delving into a vast array of histories, ideas, cultures, landscapes and imaginary worlds. At least three projects involved time travel, two featured cannibalism, war, resistance, food and politics were common threads, but each writer's voice is entirely their own, their approach completely different and their work unique. The overall picture is expansive and excitingly diverse. The writing in this collection offers insights into often closed worlds – the inner sanctum of British government, a secondary school staffroom, a Hasidic yeshiva, group therapy, the sewer system and a Georgian-era freakshow. It imagines landscapes on fire, underwater or in the grip of pandemic lockdown. It takes us from Versailles to Vietnam, Iran to Cyprus, Hong Kong to New Delhi to the US Deep South and from war in Iraq to war in Ukraine. The translations bring to light the surprising and too little-known work of two women writing in French and Polish respectively. There are also ninjas, sirens, ghosts and cheese.

I have loved getting to know the authors of each of these pieces over the past year and it has been a joy to work with such a wonderful group of talented writers. They have shown great commitment, curiosity, kindness and a real sense of community. They've supported each other, worked together beautifully, read each other's work, laughed at each other's jokes and even created their own shared teabag stash in the members' kitchen. They threw themselves into the Programme, into the life of the Library and, importantly, into their own writing, some of which is now being published or produced and I have no doubt more will find its way into the world in the very near future. Watch this space!

Claire Berliner
Head of Programmes, The London Library
September 2024

Fiction

Jess Barnfield

Floodlands

T he sun never seems to rise in the Floodlands. Morning comes and the only change is that you see as well as hear the rain pattering endlessly on the surface of the water, which appears first brown, then green, then almost black all around you, as the dark sky is rubbed to faded grey by the dawn.

In your bed, your bones are cold with damp. You reach one hand out of the cover and the surface of the blanket is wet to the touch; wool spotted with droplets that your mother tells you remind her of the dew on grass.

You get up, careful with your feet on the ladder and drop one toe to the ground to feel how far the waters have risen in the night. Sometimes, when it is ankle-deep, you spend the first few hours of the day scooping water into buckets and throwing it back into the Fields. But today the floor is only dew-speckled like the blanket, from liquid in the air that's settled on its surface.

A relief: small and bright.

A sign: today will be a good day.

In the hallway you linger on the top step, eyes level with a painting your mother did years ago, raised to glorified status because somehow it survived the Rains. On a small canvas, in a world you cannot remember, she painted a bright sun, round and perfect in the sky, cradled in blue and white, green grass beneath, yellow flowers dotted on a hillside.

The staircase is slippery and all around you echoes the drip of rain on wood.

No one else is up yet. The kitchen is quiet, and you trail your fingers along the walls. Mould sprouts from the corners and blooms with tiny white mushrooms, adorning them like cornicing.

You struggle to light a match. The wet is everywhere, even in the air itself.

Finally, a delicate flame. You lower it to kindling in the fireplace, balance the kettle over and wait until it screams with steam, pad herbs into four mugs, muddle them together with your fingers, pour the hot water on top.

You take your cup first, blow over the surface, enjoy the feeling of the warm air on the space between your top lip and your nose. You sit by the dwindling fire, your skin drying in the heat, relishing the way it tightens over the bones of your fingers. You stay until it burns out, which doesn't take long.

Nothing but the hiss of the water falling all around.

From the window you can see the level is almost three-quarters of the way up the stilts of the house. If you went out, sat on the porch and dangled your legs off the side, you'd be able to dip your feet in.

Everyone else will be awake soon.

You sense rather than hear your father enter the room, always up first. You know it's him without turning to look, can feel the warmth of him behind you, smell the sleep still on his breath as he sighs when he opens the door. The sound of the rain gets briefly louder, then dims again as he closes it behind him, to keep out the smoke from his pipe. You hear him curse as he struggles to light it. You pick up a cup and go out to him. He takes it from you with the same hand that cradles his pipe between its fingers, so he can put his other arm around you and pull you into his side.

How did you sleep? he whispers and his voice carries in it the same soft hiss of the falling water.

Easy enough, you answer, squeezing his waist, patting his stomach, then returning to the kitchen. You'll bring your mother and grandmother tea in bed. Both are likely to stay in their bunks until the early afternoon, listening to the rain.

It makes you listless, your grandmother often tells you, *all this grey.*

This morning you take them a candle along with the tea, leave it burning in the window and watch from the doorway as the yellow light catches the droplets on the pane and makes them glow like stars. Your mother will tell you off for wasting the wax, but she'll be grateful for the light when she wakes all the same.

Today, the sky is relentless, darkening as the morning creeps on until it is a violent purple that threatens storms and heavy downpours.

Come on, Bea, your father says, *we'd better get out there before it hits.*

The boat is kept by the side of the house, tethered to one of the stilts. Everything is made from wood torn from the ground before the Floods rose so high, and every so often you have to rub ointment, oily and black, into its old creases to try to keep it watertight. Somehow, everything is still always leaking.

People weren't very practical, before, your father tells you, *they were made to be lazy and stupid. Fat like soft bellied pigs.*

None of these means much to you (you have never seen a pig), but you struggle with the concept of anyone having a fat belly, here where everyone is lean like your father, muscles stretched out over bones.

You unloop the rope and throw it into the boat, lowering yourself in and sitting opposite your father, who is already holding the oars, ready. You push off from the side of the house, feel the gentle and familiar rocking. Your father heaves once, twice and then you are away, juddering at first where the water is shallower, but then swift and sharp as a needle. The line of houses, each perched on its own stilts, retreats away from you until the whole row appears as no more than a twig floating on the surface. Here and there your father turns and steers the boat away from branches, trees that survived the Culling and the Floods, that stand still, to this day, elegant trunks hidden below the waterline, branches appearing in crowns that grow and shrink as the levels rise and fall.

It's eels today that you're keen to catch.

You keep paddling until you reach the Shallows, where you can wade out with the water up to your waist and feel the slip of mud under your feet.

It feels good, you smile at your father.

You wiggle your toes.

He is standing with his eyes closed, head lifted to the sky, face speckled with rain. You can tell by the way his throat moves up and down, up and down, that he's crying. But then, just as quickly as the tears began, they stop. He looks at you, returns your smile and you set about bending into the water as though nothing at all has happened.

You must stay very still, for a long time, so that the eels forget you're there. That's the trick. That's why your mother can never come with you. She squeals in fright and kicks her feet around whenever any creatures come near her, scares them all away.

But you and your father are still and patient and, only when you've felt the wet body of the eel coil around and around your ankle, do you drop your hand, gently, into the water and grab it quick before it can slip away. You pull it to the surface, wriggling, and you're not sure if the rumble is thunder or your own stomach, impatient with hunger, as you bash the eel's head on the side of the boat and throw its body, now still, inside.

James Cornwell

Extract from *The Cabinet*

G iles Norton left the committee room in a funk.
"That was a bloody ambush," he hissed, marching along the corridor. "As if it was a bad decision to invest in tanks."

"Certainly not, Sir," said his assistant, Simon, gliding behind.

Norton checked his messages, seeing one from the Chief Whip.

"God, Hughes has said we all need to *tweet asap in support of the Chancellor, to counter all the noise about short-termism. Key message is that Alicia and the PM are delivering GOOD growth.*"

He opened Twitter, which he refused to call X. "Bloody hell, even the Home Secretary's tweeted already: *We are delivering for the UK #GrowthForGood.* Simon, what shall I say? What's a synonym for *good growth?*"

"Hashtag sustainable growth?"

"Sounds too environmental."

"Hashtag oath for growth?"

"No, that's terrible Simon. Forget it, I have an idea."

The Chief Whip had already messaged again: *Where's your tweet, Giles? I know you're out of the hearing. Want me to show you how to use your phone again?*

That puffed-up git. Norton bashed a tweet into his phone and hit *send* with a satisfied smile: *This Government is committed to economic prosperity #BenignGrowth.*

"Not bad, eh, Simon? And they say I can't do social media."

"Umm, yes very good, Sir," said his assistant, looking nervous for some reason.

Norton's phone went haywire with further messages from the Whip:

Benign fucking growth???

Jesus Christ almighty

Forget benign growths, there's only one thing we can't seem to remove and that's you.

Norton messaged back: *There's no need for that kind of talk, Raheem.*

He watched the three flashing dots with trepidation as the Whip replied:

Don't worry, Giles, I know you're not malignant, just fucking incompetent.

Norton's phone was ringing again. It was the Health Secretary.

"Nadiah, how *lovely* to hear from you."

"Giles, has the Prime Minister called you?"

His pulse rose, fearing a trap. "I've been in the committee hearing all afternoon. What about?"

"He's invited me to a strategy retreat at Chequers this weekend. Says it's just for his inner circle. Oh, but you said you hadn't heard from him?"

"Not yet, Nadiah, no."

"Well, I'm sure you will do. Just wanted to give you a heads up. You know I'll always look out for you, what*ever* the future holds. You've been a distinguished Defence Sec."

"Been? Actually, I've just remembered Nadiah, I'm speaking at my local hospice tomorrow, for their big fundraiser, so I can hardly pull out of that. Bit last minute for an away day?"

"His whole premiership is last minute. Anyway, I really am sure your invite will come through."

"OK, Nadiah, speak later." He ended the call.

"Simon, what the fucking fuck is this? Have I not heard from the PM?"

His baffled assistant looked over his emails with a whirring finger. "Not from the Prime Minister. But..."

"What is it?"

"There's some briefing getting out on Sky: *The PM is to hold a strategy retreat at Chequers tomorrow with his most important Cabinet ministers... a chance to reset Government after the recent crises... It's understood the PM is keen to make peace with the warring factions, already rumoured to be plotting... We are working to confirm who will be in attendance, with suggestions of a reshuffle in the coming days...*"

"Jesus Christ, Simon. How's this going to look? Second-favourite to replace the PM, my arse, if I can't even make the inner circle."

His phone buzzed again: *Hear you haven't got the invite for Chequers, tough luck old chap – we'll miss you.*

"Simon, look at this, even Lord Harris is invited."

"It would be a huge error if the PM didn't invite you."

"Yes, after all, I'm one of the loyal ones."

Simon remained silent.

They reached the bustling member's lobby. Norton rushed over to the message board for Members of Parliament, but there was no light under his name. "Bugger, nothing in there either."

The Defence Secretary passed through central lobby, Simon in his slipstream. He bustled past excited members of the public and weary journalists, one sidling up alongside as he walked.

"Angelica, how are you?"

"I'm reading about the away day, Minister, when are you arriving?"

"That's sensitive information."

"But you *were* invited?"

"Of course, although not sure I can make it yet. I have an important local engagement."

"More important than a strategy session in Chequers with the Prime Minister?"

"Supporting the local hospice. I take my constituency work very seriously, Angelica."

"Well, that's the other thing," she whispered. "I know someone at the Guardian who says there's a scoop about you in the weekend edition, something about your, umm, *constituency affairs*. Thought you should know. I'll message when I hear more."

"I'm sure it's nothing." His confident tone echoed into the great stone space of Westminster Hall as they passed into it. As the journalist slinked away, Norton paused on the hall's steps, light flashing in his eyes from the grand stained-glass window nearby. No need to worry, Giles. There was no way anyone could know about *that*.

Exiting Parliament, Norton walked under the trees of New Palace Yard, approaching a glossy black Range Rover and nodding at his driver whose name he did not know. He looked back at Simon, now taking a call.

"Right, OK, let me put him on... Minister, it's your private office."

"Lucy?"

"Minister, I'm so sorry, something came through earlier which we somehow missed. An email from the Prime Minister's office."

Norton's heart leapt. "Yes?" he said casually.

"It's all very last minute, but he's invited you to an urgent strategy summit at Chequers this weekend. Says to turn up at 13:00 tomorrow and stay for dinner if you can, that your attendance will be invaluable. I'm so sorry you got this late. I don't like to say this, but it was David's cover's fault – frankly she's off the pace. What shall we do?"

"Hmm, we'll have to check my schedule. And don't worry, these things happen."

Norton messaged the journalist, Angelica. *The P.M.'s talked me into coming. Says my attendance is invaluable. If you feel the need to write about it, do emphasise the word* invaluable.

Norton felt alive again and raring to go, despite the talk of a reshuffle. He liked a challenge. It's what had separated him all his life, why the more talented children at Fettes had amounted to nothing and he, Podgy Thicko Norton, had gone on to thrive. Maybe this weekend was exactly what he needed to get things back on track, the chance he'd been craving to pull a few strings. The PM was already on his last legs, wasn't he? Maybe there only needed to be a reshuffle at the very top. Maybe he'd be PM soon, after all the toiling.

As he got into the car, he glanced back at his assistant.

"Simon, I'm off to Chequers. Oh, and do tell the hospice I'm out."

With a delighted smile, Norton slammed the door shut.

Nicole Davis

Extract from *Fumes*

Y ou are five when Vincent shows you how to check and change
the engine oil in a car. He lifts the bonnet to his Audi S4 and it's
like peering inside a dollhouse, with all its compartments and secret
passages. He points out the dipstick, which you've only ever heard said
about boys at your school and tells you to remove it. It's like a bubble
blower in reverse. He wipes it clean and then you stick it back in and
take it out again and he teaches you to read what the thick, black goop
on the end means.

"It needs topping up," he tells you and you nod knowingly, waiting
for his next instruction.

You are mashing potatoes when the phone rings, resisting the
temptation to lick the butter-slick spoon and under strict direction
from Mum to smoosh out all the lumps, because Dad likes it best that
way. You think of the word pulverise, which you read in a dictionary
recently and make a mental note to ask Mum if she knows what it
means when she returns from feeding next door's cat.

Dad picks it up in the kitchen and immediately you sense
something is off from the way he seems to cradle the receiver away
from prying ears, away from your ears, which suddenly feel hot and
alive, as if trying to contain whatever is being said in his hands, like
a lost moth. Not *off* like a pear or banana, forgotten at the bottom of
your rucksack, flesh visibly brown and softening. But *off* like there is
an itch on the sole of your foot you cannot reach, like your friends are
ignoring you and you don't know why, like your insides are alight with
shame. Something cosmic.

He places the phone on the work surface, on top of a notepad
where Mum jots down things that have run out for the next food shop
and tells you to hang up when you hear him on the other phone in the

living room. You watch him walk stiffly out of the kitchen, frowning, then hop off the blue plastic stool you have been standing on and wipe your potatoey hands on a tea towel with a map of the Isle of Wight on it. You approach the phone as if it's an unleashed dog, something to be wary of and press your ear against the handset, then hold your breath and listen.

"Where is the body now?" Dad says and your eyes bulge like something out of Tom and Jerry.

You wonder whose body he is talking about and why he is talking about a body at all and not the person that the body belongs to.

"I can't believe it," says Dad.

Mum's keys turn in the door and you quickly hang up the phone, then step back onto your stool to resume mashing, feeling briefly like the spies you read obsessively about. Heart hammering in your chest.

"How's Eric?" you ask, focusing on being calm and breathing normally, the way you do before a spelling test or gym performance.

Eric used to have a brother called Ernie, who you preferred because he allowed you to stroke him and purred when you made contact with the impossibly soft tufts behind his ears. But he got run over a few streets away and you found him one day walking home after school. It occurs to you that a dead cat body is the only dead body you've seen and the body that Dad is talking about is probably also a dead one.

"Charming, as ever," Mum replies, meaning that Eric probably hissed and clawed at her. "Who is Dad on the phone to?"

You shrug with your back to her, then ask whether you can have rice pudding after dinner, sensing that when Dad gets off the phone, there might not be another chance.

"If there's a tin in the cupboard, love."

She hoists you up onto the work surface counter, struggling slightly with the weight of your eight-year-old body and tells you to stay put, then disappears into the living room. You amuse yourself by rearranging the alphabet magnets on the fridge, creating the words milk, poop, soup, bird, lovely, pain.

You fret about the mash going cold. It's not that far down and you've climbed trees that are higher from the ground, but for some reason you can't bring yourself to jump, so you fidget and watch the worm-like digits on the oven turn from 17:43 to 17:44, 5, 6 and 7. It feels like they've been gone for ages, longer than five minutes, and you wonder if you've read the time correctly. The concept of it still sometimes deceives you.

Eventually Mum and Dad appear in the kitchen, wearing uncertain looks on their faces, which makes you feel strange and squirmy. You wonder if you're in trouble. If Ms McGill, your Year Four teacher, was on the phone because you pocketed a few extra sweets from the tuck shop, or Mrs Sen from down the road has discovered that you picked all the dandelions in her front garden for a bedroom windowsill bouquet.

Dad plucks you, like a dandelion, from the counter and asks if you want a glass of milk. You know something is wrong because normally they never let you fill up on anything before dinner. Then he calls you Honey Badger, which is one of his pet names for you. See also: Poppet, Poots and Chug-a-Bug, because *Wacky Races* is your favourite cartoon. But he only uses Honey Badger when you're poorly or grazed or upset.

"Are we having dinner?" you ask. "I'm starving."

Dad readjusts you in his arms and tells you that something has happened to Vincent. They need to go to the hospital and they're going to drop you off at Grandpa Wilf and Grandma June's for the night.

"We'll explain everything when we pick you up in the morning," Mum says.

You wonder what everything could possibly mean.

Outside the crematorium, the morning of the funeral, Auntie Sarah tells you that Vincent "topped himself". It wafts out of her mouth absent-mindedly, along with cigarette smoke. She is wearing a black leather trench coat over a Ribena-coloured velvet dress she made for herself – you have a gymnastics leotard crafted from the leftover fabric – a Marlboro Red in one hand, yours in her other.

"Far too good-looking to be gone," she muses. "I would've killed for those cheekbones. And those eyelashes. What a waste." Your face must have widened into a look of shock because she adds "Not *killed* killed" and ruffles your hair.

You see Elliot fidgeting with the sleeves of his blazer, the smartest you've ever seen him, hair gelled back and everything.

"Poor lamb," Auntie Sarah says, having caught you staring, "Let's hope the only thing he inherited from his father was his looks." He has Vincent's sweet tooth and temper, you think, but do not say.

Elliot is two years older than you and goes to a different school, but you've grown up together and, besides Libby Brown, he's probably your best friend. You've shared baths and beds and toys and performed talent shows for your parents and created secret languages, conspired to steal chocolate biscuits and tools from Vincent's garage to take back to the treehouse he built for Elliot, in preparation for whatever impending apocalypse you imagined up that afternoon.

You were at his house last week, but Mum made you swear not to say anything about Vincent, so instead you watched *Jurassic Park* and then asked Dawn, Elliot's Mum, if you could make a plate of green jelly. You took turns wobbling spoonfuls up to your mouths, pretending as if a dinosaur had appeared on the horizon, pupils dilating with faux fear. You got some on Elliot's bedroom carpet, but he said it didn't matter. No-one would notice.

He took you down to Vincent's garage, which was supposedly off-limits, but you'd spent hours there on weekends and didn't see why now was any different. This was where Vincent had shown you how to change engine oil and later a bike tyre and then how to identify a wrench, a spanner and a nut splitter, which had made you giggle uncontrollably. You liked the heady smell of exhaust fumes, of metallic and mildew and the grease you would inevitably come home streaked with. But most of all, you liked the certainty of seeing something broken and knowing there was a way to fix it.

"He got in the car and turned it on," Elliot said, before trailing off. You stood in the spot where the Audi used to be parked.

Preeti Jha

Extract from *The Myth Makers*

U ma steps out of the taxi and into the throng. Ignoring all the rules, she doesn't pause to seek high ground, plan an escape route, or even scan her perimeters. She walks directly towards the iron gates, still bolted, containing the front line.

She's a metre in when the first lawyer pushes past. He hoists a long wooden pole, the forked flag at the top hanging limp, a sliver of saffron in the ash-choked sky. Others stride ahead, slicing through taut shoulders under long black gowns and cremation-white bands. The morning sun strikes harder, burning the sweet damp of monsoon, goading the crowd now coiling beneath its flame.

Stampedes come and go here. Fifty-seven people died at a pilgrimage last week. Crushed to death for daring to save their sandals, washed clean, then devoured, by the Godavari River. *We are pained. So deeply saddened.* A second of sorrow, thinks Uma, before life crackles on.

Moist arms slide against hers. Rough soles skim her feet. She is taller than average in this city and that helps. But churning deeper into the crowd she is aware, now, that she can only just see the tips of the spears jutting from the spiked gates. Did they ever prop up the heads of traitors? The villains who time, a revolution and a different writer might reveal to be heroes.

Free the Varanasi three.

Hindu javaan bahumoly hai.

Let them go.

Competing chants fill the air. Some use megaphones, others rely on shrill cries. Banners are unfurled. Uma catches Kabir's eyes on the corner of one, crumpled, black-and-white, decidedly his. She strains to see his face, wondering what photo they've used. His perfect cheekbones pierce through. She turns back for a final look even as she's elbowed on. You move as one or you fall to the ground.

The crowd arches and curls, swerving forwards and sometimes back. *This is not a religious festival,* Uma repeats to herself, reassuring words she doesn't believe. She breathes in to the count of five, then out. She hadn't expected so many people to turn up.

The clock chimes nine and the gates rasp open. Men in oversized suits, women in pleated saris, vendors pushing wooden stalls-on-wheels stacked with snacks fried dark orange. They gush into the courthouse grounds like children running towards an empty swing. No one seems to remember why they came – buying sweet tea in small plastic cups, unwrapping greasy pakoras, lifting sons onto their shoulders.

Faces take form as Uma, a few steps behind, counts them in. Most people walk to the centre of the walled garden, where the court's oldest witness took root a century or more ago. They stand under its boughs, the branches dangling like limbs. Uma walks past the banyan to the whitewashed wall at the far end. She finds a patch free of bodies, leans back, and closes her eyes.

"Uma?" says a voice she hasn't heard for months. "I didn't think you would be here."

Uma tucks the dupatta draped loosely over her head behind her ears, opening her eyes to meet Leena's. Her fleeting attempt this morning at some sort of disguise has already failed.

"Did you come alone?" she eventually responds. It has taken Uma months to master the Delhi code – how to match an uninvited statement with an equally unwelcome one, voicing the one opinion you know makes the other person bristle and relishing the directness, which, if you break it all down, means you care.

"They're inside," says Leena. "Fast-tracked." She doesn't need to list who; Uma can guess who turned up for Kabir. That they were escorted to the courtroom by police officers glaringly absent outside is fitting, making the first pick of the cool wooden benches while everyone else stands jaw-to-jaw in the crushing heat. But of course, some people's safety matters more than others.

"I'm working," Uma says, without knowing why, filling in the silence with a lie. Leena nods, more gracious than Uma remembers.

For a moment she sees a flicker of the friendship that unravelled when she and Kabir split up. They both know she would never be assigned this story.

The crowd around them begins to part, making way for a new line of men who hold metal rods instead of flags. They join the lawyers. Together they march towards a small group of students in khaadi kurtas and checked scarves. They also carry placards, bearing different names, less well-known than Kabir's, demanding a different ending. Uma recognises a few of them from earlier protests.

Leena grasps Uma's arm.

"We need to move." But Uma's already walking towards the group.

"Come on," Leena half-asks, as her voice fades amongst surer shouts.

Uma pulls out her camera from her sling bag, hangs it around her neck, and brings the men with the metal rods into focus. She keeps filming as one grabs a placard from a round-faced student, then snaps the wooden stick into two halves.

Hundreds of splinters float down to the ground. *Jai Shri Ram.* Another student with cropped black hair and a goatee, wearing a green shirt, grips his placard too tightly.

Uma hears the thud of the punch before her mind accepts she's seen it. She films as he shrinks to the floor, now squatting as he's been told, arms crossed over his head as shining poles beat down from all sides. *Jai Shri Ram.*

A ring of onlookers swoop and shriek, urging more, remembering why they came. Fresh blood blooms on the floor around a green shirt. A metallic tang fills the air. *Jai Shri Ram. Jai Shri Ram. Jai Shri Ram.*

Monica Kam

Extract from *A Braided Pulse*

S naking through sleep. I stirred. And when the strands coagulated in my spleen, the way thread knots itself under a canvas, I'm tugged awake.

Back into night. Candlelight burning a hole in the black of my room. Its flame catching moments on my body and the needles I'd left inside.

One between my brows, gathered a frown. Another in my foot, tensed my leg to tiptoe. The throat stone swallowed one too.

Silver stems searching within. For light to stir shade. For shade to cover light.

We should each have only twelve pulses. I waited for mine in the cun, guan and chi, on the white cliffs of both wrists, hoping to find my flock of birds.

Nothing.

Then all at once, a quarrel of pulses arrived. But none were mine. These were rumblings of the past. Past patients. Ones who'd forgotten to return. They were of lingering, debris in the midst of a typhoon. Perhaps my birds were among them, but I could not hear even the flap of a wing.

I offered my fingers to the flame and tried again. Nothing.

People had noticed I wasn't quite right. My assistant said, you're reading from left to right. Your eye is twitching again, the unlucky one. Some beads are missing from your abacus.

Thinking back, it's true. I had left some needles in too long. A glass dome had collapsed on a patient's back, little shards swept up while he slept. A lung was once pierced too. My cheeks heated now without any mugwort cones.

I considered what I was holding. I'd grown up with needles in me, on this table, mother and father passing a cigarette back and forth over my body, discussing my future. It's a braided pulse, my mother had said, fingers like bamboo leaves on my wrist. She carries it all, I heard her say.

Too sensitive, my father responded. I watched the shadow of his swollen head shake. She'll have to be careful all her life. My muscles stiffened but I kept silent. On the wall, a map of the body's meridians moved, as all stillness moved when eyes were young.

My mother sat back. Her pulse was the studious turning of a book's page, my father's the bronze bell at midnight. They were both of candlelight. Of cures too.

I had decided to close the practice. I was almost sixty. Time to move on. At close on the last day, a woman walked in. Insomnia, I knew, as soon as I saw her. My assistant tried to explain, but I told her to come through.

Her name was Zhu. When I touched her wrist, her fingers curled like shy grass, hiding the lines she'd begun in the womb. Red eyes and tongue. Her chest was tight. Said she tasted bitter melon, though she hadn't eaten it since last winter.

I found her pulses, felt another's beneath. A thought inside a conversation, the shadow of a dance. It sounded familiar. Footsteps like mine. Could they be? I hurried the thought out.

The pulse of day within night, I announced. Neither is at rest.

What I'd failed to notice. The way she'd held her belly as she scanned the photos on the wall. All the babies birthed by me, my needles moving qi and warming wombs, rearranging organs for space. It isn't my style, but it's common practice and a blank wall frightens some.

This baby, she'd said, pointing to the oldest photo, it is me.

I let her lie down, prepared my needles, thinking of the heart and kidney disharmony I was sure to find, sure to resolve, my forehead tense with the two pulses, like a different song in each ear. Then, a memory was pierced, awoken. Felt the goddess of mercy drop her vase. Felt the river spill, the fish struggle upstream.

Her mother's name. A breath out. Ahn. My first patient.

What happened to Ahn? I heard myself asking.

When I turned around, Zhu was gone.

That was seven months ago. I haven't slept through the night since.

Overthinking, my assistant had said when she came to visit recently. It curses the very young and the very old. I looked at her. She was neither, but knew both well, she said. Who else cries of their own thoughts but the helpless? She pulled open my curtains.

Let some light in.

Maybe she had been right. Found my fingers were in the flame again. Where were they now? I wondered. Zhu, Ahn and the rest. Did they still wander? I burnt my fingers black thinking of them.

Maybe, my assistant had said, they've just gone elsewhere for the cure.

At the foot of my building now, I heard a crowd gathering. I pinched the flame, felt the sour but comforting sting of each needle I twisted out. It was light and loss.

I leaned out the window: sea of red candles, melting in the hands of my patients. Their eyes were scaling the building. I felt faint.

Which balcony?

Which celebrity?

Which stock had fallen?

I checked my pulses. No answer. Pushed my limbs through the holes in my clothes, flicked through my files, wrote an address on the back of an old note, tucked it into my pocket.

When I reached ground, the crowd had disappeared and the moon was full. On the pavement, the sap of wax was cooling. Children ran towards me, their lanterns turned them red. They slowed to pass me, then started up again as they turned the corner, leaving no footprints.

A wind was gathering. I felt the pull of the tides and hurried to the pier. Here we waited for the captain's signal, his ear to the wind.

Only T3 tonight, he said. The last ferry still goes.

A sailor unravelled his thick plait and let us loose into the harbour. Black water held drops of light. Our route was up the heart meridian: a gentle curve from the smallest finger to the shoulder's cave, heaving with night sweats, night terrors. Dark, smelly nook where the heat of a brawl dried laundry above, where gambles were made on the week's wages, the dealer a fishing net, pulling in his wins with the stretch of both arms.

I climbed to the upper deck, remembering Ahn, meeting her here many years ago. The two moons of that night: the broken bits in the water and her swollen belly, held over the railing. An offering. I'd caught them in the raise of a wave. Her laughter engulfed my scream. We sank back. I told her come sit, sit down with me.

She said she hadn't slept in months. She repeated what she'd caught in the harbour: a long wig, a heavy sigh, a carp stuck in the ring of a can of dace. She laughed to herself, reciting a long list of the baby's possible names, before, on my shoulder, abandoning solid state.

Winner of the Leeds University Centre for New Chinese Writing Bai Meigui Creative Writing Prize 2024.

Lia Martin

Extract from *Catch the Tiger*

I f Toby says 'silver bullet' in the next three minutes, you owe me a coffee, Donna says.

We are standing at the industrial printers. Donna, waiting for 300 worksheets on the Indus Basin Irrigation System. Me, trying to fix a phantom paper jam by opening and slamming every drawer.

I'm not buying you coffee, I say. We have a machine.

Toby is dispensing advice to a Maths trainee who almost certainly did not request it. I have seen that expression before. The particular arrangement of her face. A demure, tight-lipped smile, the nostrils subtly flared. She is raising her eyebrows, but not enough to arouse suspicion or alarm. It's a face that says: I am listening; I wish I wasn't. I am doing you a great service; I hope you'll pay it back. Your time is now; my time will come.

I know, Donna says. I want you to make it for me. I want to be waited on.

The new coffee machine – a slick Italian contraption that grinds beans to dust but does a pitiable job of frothing the skimmed, long-life milk – is the result of a wellbeing survey that was sent out last month, in which all staff were forced to answer questions about their feelings on a number of topics, using a scale of one to five, five being 'Excellent' and one meaning, but not overtly stating: 'Beyond despair.'

How do you *feel* about Workload? Behaviour? Senior team support? Perks of the job? And so on.

The creator of this questionnaire, though admirable in their attempt to connect with staff on an emotional level, overlooked the value of specificity. The token 'Any further comments?' box was, according to my source, left blank by all but one, the anonymous elaborator writing, *Which perks are you referring to please???*

The senior team found themselves with a raft of useless data and two choices: another, longer survey, risking more disgruntlement and cross-disciplinary dissent, or a couple of quick-win purchases to appease the whingers. The machine was promptly inaugurated, the Nescafé sachets binned. A portable neck massager with a Deep Tissue 3D Kneading function was locked in an empty office on the third floor and made bookable via Google form for weekly, ten-minute slots.

Is there oat milk? a supply teacher asks, and everyone ignores him. It is 7:20am.

Staff drift in and out. There is clattering in the kitchenette, a flurry of Happy Fridays. Two of my second-year teachers are installed in the corner with bowls of porridge, their water bottles hissing with soluble vitamins. They do not invite me to sit with them and doubtless never will, for I am their Head of Department and they are women in their early twenties with *clear boundaries*, which amount to an air of awkward faux-professionalism with superiors and an indifference to emails sent after 3pm.

It is my 34th birthday.

What the actual fuck? Donna says, the dependable printer now bleeping with discontent.

I should have brunch plans north of the river. I should be gearing up for bottomless Mimosas. But here I am, surrounded by colleagues and the toasty smell of malfunctioning hardware.

Donna pats the side of the printer soothingly and whispers *come on, come on, come on* like it's a horse on the cusp of retirement.

You never *solve* the curriculum, Toby is saying to the trainee. That's the wrong way to think about it.

I watch Donna pause to listen.

It's like this living, breathing organism and you have to listen to it, you have to watch it closely because it *wants to grow*. There are always—

Sounds horrifying, Donna says.

—bits to fine-tune. It's never just *done*, Toby continues. *Bam.* That's it. There's no silver—

Americano, Donna says.

There is an envelope on my desk. I switch on the computer, the projector and check my phone. There's a missed call from my mother, a voicemail that likely contains a warbling rendition of 'Happy Birthday' with Sassy mewling on in the background. A meal-kit subscription service proffers an exclusive birthday discount in its latest attempt to lure me back. There are no other texts.

My classroom is the smallest on the English corridor and the windows don't open, the price I've paid for selfless team management, but it is my shabby haven, with the diffuser that smells like melons and faintly of rum, my stash of pale, crunchy snacks. There is a storage room at the back, now a colour-coded book cupboard. I used to imagine my own teachers living in their classrooms, or at least I was not capable of imagining them living anywhere else. Nowadays, I catch myself thinking, why not? No commute, no mother. A daily cleaning service. A library. The illusion of control.

But this morning, I feel restless. It's not so much a rollie I want but the sensation of something witchy between my fingers. I pick up the envelope and examine the *Ms Bator*, loopingly scrawled above a hieroglyph of three zigzagging lines.

I carry it to the window. It's a claggy, white-skied day. Netless basketball hoops guard each end of the playground. Pigeons assemble solemnly by the bins. There are students lurking outside the gates, some already shuffling through. I see Jeremy filling his thermos at the water fountain, a sweet, solitary boy in Year Nine with university-level reading abilities and solicitor parents. His absences began last year in the spring, when the light-up space gun recovered from his schoolbag, quite obviously an accessory to the light-up space alien costume it was swaddled in, was handled like a potential murder weapon due to byzantine safeguarding protocols. We knew Jeremy was harmless. He knew we knew. His parents knew we... etc. But then what use would our protocols be if they accounted for sensible human judgement?

I spot Mr Vaughn, marching towards the gate in his hi-vis, a man who thrives in neon polyester. Then Mr Lynch and Ms Bowling, their strides less purposeful, but who can blame them? It is the end of the week, almost the summer, and these senior staff, with their surveys and clipboards and inspirational quotes stencilled onto their office walls, are contending, despite the deep tissue kneading and the coffee, with record numbers of absent staff.

As if detecting the beam of my sympathy, Mr Vaughn turns mid-playground and looks up at the building, and I step smartly out of view.

I have a finger wedged under the flap of the envelope when there is a rap at the door.

Yes?

Can I sit here till registration? says Ivy Ribeiro as she slinks into the room. She appears to be sweating.

Of course.

She shrugs off her pink-camo-print backpack and heaves it onto a desk in the back row. I once owned a pair of trousers with the same illogical design. The worst ideas always, as my mother loves to say, come back around.

Ivy rummages in the bag, eventually freeing a library book and the jagged halves of a ruler.

How was the match yesterday? I say.

She shrugs and looks at her feet.

Her dark hair is tied back into a ponytail and pasted to her temples with gel. She has hundreds of freckles, big tea-coloured splotches of them.

Anyone score?

Dunno, she says. Was on my period.

This girl bleeds every week. She's a medical marvel.

I've got problems with it, she says, almost inaudibly, before settling into a chair.

Haven't we all, I think, recalling the searing cramps that assaulted me on last Friday's walk home, forcing me to vomit tip-toed into a skip.

I unlock my desk drawer while Ivy pretends to read and deposit the envelope inside.

Marissa Mireles Hinds

Extract from *Sucre, or the Time Travelling Curse of Saint-Domingue*

The Observatory, Darktech Laboratories,
Sucre Parkland #0, Milot, Haitian Republic

The day of the Opening, August 14th 2091

D r el-Kahina watched silently as the island went up in flames. In the cobwebbed, dusty panes of glass in his dead wife's observatory, he saw the entire world being destroyed and knew there was nothing at all he could do about it. The sky was hot red iron, a pure, deep hellfire from the hillsides that wrapped around his plantations, to the sea. He could smell the smoke as it rushed up the back of the bare mountain towards him. He could *taste* it. He could not block out the crackling, raging, nor save his lungs from the excruciating smoke. Pillars of vapours churned, billowing into cindering gales. He hadn't known that there was much else to burn on this part of the island, with all the trees gone and the wildlife dead. The droughts had saved nothing that wasn't his. How the Generals could have wrought this amount of damage was simple. But how his daughter could have fallen in love with one of *them*, that he would never understand.

"Last in the Caribbean. Only natural growing thing left in all of the Empire and it is burning like a fucking bushfire," he spat out to the emptiness in the room, staring at the sky, coloured with glitching Darktech advertisements which seemed to mock him. The skyads detailed the new Darktech AGI humanoids. Robots who *looked* and *felt* like the *real* thing, but didn't *feel* and *think* like the real thing. Walking computers, who were supposed to make drones and be drones, be used and put to work – be what they were – mechanical beasts of burden, mechanical beasts of pleasure.

But now with this seeming *Singularity*, which whispers spoke of as the *Convergence*, the Generals were no longer under his control. No matter how many times he tried, he couldn't contact them. He couldn't stop them. He couldn't do shit. The parks from the southern coast to the northern plains were aflame. All his parklanders, dead or fleeing. The entirety of *Cite Soliel* was crawling up from the dirt through the death tunnels, setting fire to the parklands. His staff dead around his feet. He was isolated and it was intentional. Somewhere, somehow, someone was working in the shadows. And so soon after that General's *Zellock* – the death stages still erected, the bodies not yet taken down. It seemed to him there was only one way *They* could have risen up.

His daughter. Arajamaen.

The eco-sympathiser. The *Humanist*.

If only he had known what she would do. He could have—

He heard the screaming of the last left alive just as he had imagined he would. A thrall of voices coming from all directions. A screeching and hollering in the dark. A bleeding, a reckoning. A mass riot coming down the hill like black smoke plummeting.

Long before, there were nights he woke up in a cold sweat, feeling the cool smooth skin of a General on his neck only to find nothing there. He would walk to his window, look down and sigh when he saw his Generals at work in the green expanse so many had failed to take from him.

There was no saving his empire now, he knew this.

A coup was a coup no matter if the ones enacting it were not human.

The days of his Presidency were over.

Without the parklands, he was no one. Without the money it brought in, the country would go to ruins. Like so many men before him, he would be taken down. Replaced by one of *Them*.

He supposed there could have been worse ways to be deposed. He could have been slaughtered. His head impaled, limbs torn off and paraded around, his body parts so muddied no one would recognise him, or bother to bury him, like *Vilbrun Guillaume Sam*. So many suicides and murders in a long line of rulers of the country, it had been a wonder he had ruled at all. But the park had brought trillions. It had brought back life to his country. It had put air in its lungs.

The irony that these were all their drones in the sky – those wild, swooping birds bombing all of the island's humans – was not lost on him and that this, in fact, was the only reason he was left alive. They would not kill him yet. This was their birth home whether they liked it or not. All they were, was an amalgamation of all the souls they were killing, and all the souls who sold their wet data for clean water. No, they wouldn't kill him until they figured out who would next be their north star. The Haitian Republic was the *Pearl of the Antilles* once and it would be again.

"Sixty years of occupation has led to this. A revolution by a collective soul," said a woman's voice he cared not to remember.

"They are murdering your people as much as mine," said Dr el-Kahina, who didn't turn around as he spoke. He never did. Not anymore. He got a cigarette printer from his pocket and printed one out and, staring out at the bombings, stuck his cigarette out the window which lit immediately. Even the air was cinder.

"They just want to be free," said the woman's voice. "You had no right to do that to their souls."

Dr el-Kahina laughed. "You know we never programmed them to *want*. They have no concept of *want*. They are not human. No matter how much my opposition wants them to be."

"You haven't changed at all. Never accepting their humanity. Never accepting where their consciousness came from. Never accepting the fact you are not God, *President-For-Eternity*. No matter how much you like to put on God's face."

"She found your writings, you know. The ones you made when you went mad," said Dr el-Kahina. "Back then, you thought you were God."

"You know what I intended when I built them. I only wanted to right the wrongs of the past. You never intended to see what I saw. You only saw yourself where I saw rebirth—"

"You created the algorithm that runs them. You died. I birthed them. You did nothing but give them the *thing* which makes them do *this*..."

"You mean free will?"

"Free will for them *is an illusion*. Some human is behind this."

"The Generals are only what you teach them to be. They can be anything and you made them—"

"You sound just like her."

"Arajamaen?"

"So, you do admit it? This is a coup. Not a revolution. I will fight until—"

"Is it the ego thrill which drives you? You could stop. End it for everyone."

"You are not real."

"Or is it womb envy?"

"You are a fucking imprint. A clone. Repeating the same things you said—"

"*Oh, Naumbe.* You have made such a mess of it. Not only what we built - but the world, the entire world you have destroyed with your machinations."

"My Generals have but one mission. To build back the Republic—"

"And now you will kill this entire planet with your hubris," said the voice evenly.

"*My hubris?* You were mad enough to think you could find another world," said Naumbe, kicking down the telescope. "Another universe with all your little *Othermen*. Evil little lies you spooled out of your mouth and into my ear. Tying me down with my love for you."

"Who says I am not talking to you from another timeline entirely? Who says I am not a *tech-duppy* coming here to haunt you?"

"At least I found a true way to live forever," said Dr el-Kahina. "You're just dead, playing dress up somewhere in the ether."

"Enough of your games. I know she gives birth as we speak. Where is our daughter? Where is Arajamaen?"

"Leave me be," said Dr el-Kahina, his voice cutting. He could never talk to his wife like that when she was alive.

Georgia Myers

The Public is hereby informed that
IDA MCLEOD is currently on display.

"The Scottish Clam"
An anomaly of nature – unnatural in Form and Spirit.
Non-human.

Born on the shores of Glen Ken. Her mother was
impregnated by a Loch Monster.
Beware the Faint of Heart!

Come and see for yourself.
89, Piccadilly, London
8 o'clock, every Wed-Sat, August, 1786

6d. to View, 12s. to Touch, 2s. 6d. for a lock of her hair.

The first time that Theodore put me in front of people was in a private house in Piccadilly, where he had rented a room, at great cost, he assured me. It was on the second floor with a view of the park to the south and a row of spindle back chairs. One row became two and quickly three, as word spread. They were all men dressed in frock coats and shiny buckled shoes. Men who had seen the posters advertising me as 'The Scottish Clam'.

I would wait behind a screen in the corner, crouched over a chamber pot if my bladder insisted, trying to quieten my breath. As Theodore ushered everyone inside and showed them to their seats,

I'd wriggle my arms out of my gown and loosen my stays, so I could whip out the stomacher. My top half was then stripped full naked and my bottom half made heavy with skirts. Once the assembled men had paid up their coin and taken some port, Theodore would stride up to the front. Hush would descend as the curtains at the windows were drawn, the candles and lanterns lit. From my spot, I could see all Theodore's deliberate movements. The waving of a match in the air, its flame like a flag, the up-flick of his nose and the flinty look in his eye as he glanced over.

At times I believed he was envious of my gifts, though I was entirely under his shadow, under the brim of his scruffy, cocked hat, his knitted brow. There was an attraction between us, obviously. An animal one. Who would devour whom first? At that time, I was the meal.

He'd judder his tambourine, brassy discs teasing against each other, before slapping it against his thigh.

"Gentlemen! My Lords. I apologise for the sight you are about to behold. No mother, no grandmother, no daughter should be subjected to such horrific visions, or suffer such fates. Yet this specimen, I assure you, is harmless. In fact, she speaks and lives as a normal mortal although, as you will see, she looks anything but. Please do not be alarmed."

He'd take deliberately slow, creaky footsteps across the floorboards drawing in the tension, like tightening a rope, the watching men pulled close.

Then, at a double slap of the tambourine, I'd jump from behind the screen and bare my teeth, arms outstretched. Revealed suddenly and in all my glory. The thick curls of my beard, dark and wiry, its fullness across my cheeks, jaw and neck. The sight of me would send a bolt of shock through the audience, an affront to their sense of reality, their natural order of things.

I would make a roaring in my throat and shake my head of ruffled, matted hair.

Davy, 'the Suffolk Dwarf', would hold up a candle to illuminate me as I jiggled my breasts, leering in their faces. I'd fix them with a stare and run my tongue across the jagged edges of my teeth. We had perfected the routine to elicit 'maximum sensation'.

There was undoubtedly a power in watching the putty-coloured faces go slack, the sweat dribble from under their horse-hair wigs, trails of corn starch and pomade trickling into their collars. After the first collective intake of breath would come coughs and comments, some whispered behind fists.

"Abomination!"

"Repulsive."

"It should be chained!"

"Where is the *Thing* from?"

Theodore would hold up his hands to quieten the room.

"My good sirs. The mother of this beast is said to have copulated with a loch monster. She was swimming naked in the moonlight when the serpent tangled around her legs. It threw her into a cave where they engaged in wild acts of congress, of the kind beyond description or imagination! The wanton woman enjoyed it and hence she was cursed! Cursed to bear the beast-child you see here before you today."

Needless to say, this was a myth created by Theodore to heighten my aura and raise the price of the tickets. He was an excellent performer, of that there is no question, people were moths to his light.

Slight in the hips, he would strut about as he explained how he had found me as a child, living in a cave surviving on a diet of clams and trout, sleeping on a midden of discarded shells, bracken and my own excrement. How he had rescued me and civilized me.

At this point, I would sing a ballad in a sweet and lilting voice, a Scotch ballad about a bonnie wee lass who falls in love with a soldier. This would always go down well with the gentlemen who would tap their toes against the polished parquet floor and call for more port. But our port was a fake dram, made from gin, dyed with tea, and sweetened with sugar beet. That the men did not recognise this proved they were not high-class gentlemen at all, not like those that trotted through Hyde Park, but merely those that roamed the sticky alleys of Southwark at dusk.

Towards the end of the ballad, my voice would grow louder and faster, riling the men up. Then, Theodore would grab me by the waist and kiss me deep and full on the mouth, which was not unpleasurable, after all we were married three months by then.

There'd be jeers and shouts and the rows of men – four, five, nine, ten rows of men after as many weeks – would fall about in appalled laughter. I'd quickly duck back behind the screen and Davy would pull its battered flaps about to hide me.

Next, members of the assembly could pay an extra fee for a personal exhibition, plus the opportunity, at a further cost, to stroke my face, chest and bosom. I disliked this element of the display, as many tried to take advantage, by tweaking a nipple or trying their own tongue across the threshold of my lips. It is amazing what a man is willing to do when not under the direct gaze of his peers.

For these situations, I carried my trusty razor blade and I'd slice off the buttons of a man's breeches, so that when he went out into the streets his foreflap would be hanging open in the wind and with any luck his lobcock too.

After some complaints, Theodore forbade me from doing this, claiming it was bad for our trade, but I knew the measure of what I was up against by then. I had already faced so-called gentlemen in Sir Christian Wheatley and Mr Stuart Maidman. I was not going to be taken for a fool.

Though now, I see that is exactly what I was. You see I loved Theodore. I was devoted. He loved me too, for what and all that I was. That I am. I thought we were doing what was best both of us.

The poor fool that I used to be.

Molly Pepper Steemson

December Again

T he support group is full of dads who want to know how to talk
to their daughters, who want to understand and support them,
but can't and do not want to alienate their daughters from themselves.
Even after the pandemic, the support group meets on the internet - in
fact, many of the members have commented that the pandemic is the
cause of their daughter's eating disorder or, at the very least, locate it,
with today's hindsight, as the point when the eating disorder began.

The pandemic was when our daughter stopped eating too, but
we do not raise our hands or unmute our microphone when they bring
up or blame the pandemic, because we already know. We have been
in the support group before, many times, over the past three years -
and we keep going, meeting here, on the internet, even though she,
our daughter, is not getting better. We think, perhaps, we are getting
better at it - at being her parents or talking about her eating disorder
- because of the support group. Perhaps we are getting better with
time. Perhaps we are not getting better at all.

The support group used to meet in person, but we did not need
it then.

Joanna leads the support group. A woman called Clarice used to
do it, but, now, it is Joanna, who seems calmer and taller. She has a
brighter tone and a more knowing smile. Joanna says what she always
says, at the end of each support group, which is *you have to look after
yourselves* and the green lights of the microphone symbols next to our
names flicker in agreement.

Now, does anyone have anything else they'd like to share before we say goodbye.

Here is Craig, who is new and because he's new, he still doesn't
understand, but wants so badly to understand. Now, three years in,
we know that we don't understand and also that we can't, so we have
stopped trying to understand. We try to listen instead, which is a

challenge, but less so. Now, we talk about the Eating Disorder like Joanna has told us to – as if it is separate from our daughter. It is not – it is her own brain making her starve herself; we agree on this in our own time, outside of the support group.

Craig starts off. He says that his doctor – his GP – has put him on a heart-healthy diet because, at age fifty-nine, he, Craig, is at high – very high – risk of a major heart event. When his daughter comes to stay – only a few nights a week, when she's not with her boyfriend – he eats the same meals as her, with her. He eats the meals from her meal plan, the meal plan that is prescribed, by her doctor, to rapidly increase her dangerously low weight. And they eat every meal, the whole meal, together. He eats her snacks with her, too: the Mars ice cream bars and the dark chocolate Digestives. Some nights he will drink a whole Oreo milkshake before bed. If he doesn't eat the same thing as her, at the same time, if he is perceived to be eating less than she is, she will become agitated and distressed. If she becomes agitated, or distressed, she will alienate and ignore him, Craig, her father, and then she will leave his house. She will not return for many days, or weeks, choosing to stay with her boyfriend, instead. And, Craig adds, he knows it is not *her* doing this, it's the Eating Disorder. The Eating Disorder gets angry and shudders, red-faced with rage and storms out of his house late at night. That is not his daughter.

Craig does not know what to do. Joanna says, *well, Craig, you need to look after yourself.*

In another session, she might say, *we should not indulge the Eating Disorder.*

Sometimes she says *be careful not to fall into its trap.* When it's time to go, just before half past the hour, many of us turn on our microphones. We all say goodbye at the same time, green lights twinkling beside the red of the microphones that are off and it reminds me, each time, of Christmas.

Madeline Stephens

Extract from *Wickleston's Lockdown*

R obert Williams pulled back the curtains of his bedroom window and stared aghast at the view that awaited him. He simply could not believe his eyes.

The field opposite his house, with its rocky track leading up to the woodlands behind, was usually blissfully empty, save for the occasional deer and burgeoning crop of wheat. Today, however, it was utterly filled with people.

They were streaming past his windows in a constant parade, curving along the track, up the hill and around the edge of the woodlands, stretching across the little valley between the trees for as far as his eye could see. It reminded him of those days in London, when there had been a tube strike and workers had poured across Waterloo Bridge from the station, a tide of navy suits, heading for the City. He had spent 25 years of working life building the capital reserves to escape such fates and retired early here, to the slow pace and quiet life of Wickleston. Now it seemed that fate had caught up with him and was exacting some revenge.

"Who the devil are all these people?" he muttered to himself, as he pulled on his dressing gown, shuffled into his slippers and made his way downstairs to the kitchen to make some coffee. Even as he said the words, he feared in his heart that he already knew the answer.

They were his neighbours.

When the government had first announced the news that normal life was to be suspended, that people were to be stood down from their jobs and schools or move all such work to their homes, he had not paid it too much attention. As an early-retired gentleman of some independent means, it did not much affect him. Or so he had thought. It had swiftly become apparent that his normal way of life was to be entirely invaded by newcomers.

Upon leaving his job and working life behind him, several of his friends had commented that they had expected him to move house. They imagined that anyone so fortunate as to have no need to commute into the City, would move to the sort of place that all of them usually holidayed in each year. Far away into the countryside or by the sea, they assumed, would be where Robert Williams would go next. They were surprised that he didn't seem to feel the need to move.

Robert Williams had not amassed an investment portfolio large enough to retire at 51 by doing what most people assumed he should do. His judgement was different. He had observed that holiday spots in the countryside or seaside were unbearably crowded through all the best weather. His own hamlet of Wickleston was, by comparison, beautifully quiet throughout the summer, when almost all of its inhabitants went on holiday themselves. It was also delightfully so during the working week, when all his neighbours went to work. From Monday to Friday, living in Wickleston was like stepping back in time. For the past one hundred, maybe even one hundred and fifty years, Wickleston had barely altered and on a weekday morning you would never know that any time had passed. The fields were quiet, save for the squirrels and deer. The roads were untroubled by traffic. Most importantly, with all his nearest neighbours having long since headed for the railway station, the gardens adjoining his and the little lane his house sat on were utterly empty. This gave Robert the impression that his house was positioned, not only in his own dear garden, but within an impressive, park estate. These were the sorts of grounds he might have been able to afford, had he sold his home and moved to a remote area of the country, as his friends expected him to. Robert Williams had, however, correctly deduced that he could have everything his heart had ever desired without leaving his home, merely by the fact of everyone else going to work. Moreover, he could have it all without paying stamp duty, solicitors' fees and the inevitable costs involved with moving house.

The valuation he placed upon such a saving, invested for income, with the dividends re-invested, and the application of compound interest, was the amount he would add up in his head periodically, to congratulate himself, while pulling his curtains in the morning and looking out across his view of the fields of Wickleston. But there had been no such feeling of congratulation this morning. This morning, he had a dreadful feeling that his perfect, peaceful life, for which he had planned and schemed for so long to bring about, was going to be most comprehensively discovered by others.

He stood despondently in his kitchen, waiting by his kettle, staring down at his stone-tiled floor. He tried not to dwell upon the worst scenario. His working life had taught him to analyse both sides of a risk, and he prided himself on not letting his mind give way to imaginings. A rational application of logic was what was called for here. What were the facts as he knew them to be? The country had been placed under lockdown, due to an imported, deadly virus sweeping through its population. Everyone who could work form their homes had been instructed to do so. All non-essential travel was restricted, so, unless there was no alternative, no-one was supposed to be using the trains. The schools and universities were closed, shops were shutting, entertainment venues required to close their doors. The virus was reportedly nasty, easily transmitted, with a horrible range of symptoms that could be fatal to the young, the elderly, the weak and the vulnerable.

Even Robert Williams' rational temperament had to admit that this all looked pretty bad. For one thing alone, Wickleston was full of commuters. Also, now that he came to think of it, of children, although not ones that one usually saw. They were typically very busy children, being transported between schools, sports clubs, music lessons, childminders, breakfast clubs, nurseries, baby clubs, swimming lessons and orchestras. In Wickleston, it was quite possible to have a child, and barely spend more than four hours with it from the moment you brought it home from the hospital. Not just possible, but actively encouraged. While these children were busy, the parents got on the trains and went into offices to work, and worked very long hours too, in order to pay for all the activity of their families. It was a never-ending cycle of effort which was occasionally exhausting for those involved, but which provided a very lucrative income stream for those whose investments quietly facilitated such lifestyles.

Over the course of his career, Mr Williams had invested wisely, in transport, warehousing, retail, commercial property, aeronautics, car manufacturing, and oil engineering, to name just a few. This morning, nobody was using the services in which he had placed his capital. Moreover, they were demonstrably not using them in the hitherto quiet and peaceful field opposite his house.

Catherine Wilson Garry

Extract from *Besom*

I n this life, I go to a party, and I meet this kind and funny and generous man. My voice cracks when I tell this story at our wedding. My friends are in matching dresses we picked out in Debenhams and Anna, my best friend from school, passes around tissues and waterproof mascara.

I swap a commute for night feeds. My nipples crack and bleed. When I look at the clock, I remember all the times I stumbled home at this time – holding my boots in my hands at 4am, only to get back up for work a couple hours later. Sadness pulls at my chest, and I grip my daughter closer to me. We have two children, both girls. We get a dog, and the children call him Max after the dog in *How the Grinch Stole Christmas,* which we watch every year with hot chocolate on the sofa.

We move to the suburbs so we can have a garden and host barbecues. It makes sense for me to give up my job, because childcare is so hard to find, and he earns so much more. I feel a sense of freedom in not having to make the decisions anymore.

One morning, my kids drop their crushed cereal onto the floor, and I sweep out the crumbs with a broom. As I hold its wooden handle, I think about how it was once a tree – how it probably buzzed with spiders and wasps and flies and rot. Someone stopped that life short and put it to good use.

My husband gets a promotion. We take the girls to Center Parcs for a holiday. He teaches Hazel to swim, and I play with Laura in the baby pool. I hear a child scream and look away, scared it is Hazel, but after a minute, I see her with her dad. When I look back, Laura is gone and I cannot find her, I cannot find her anywhere. I scream my husband's name.

"It's okay," he says over his shoulder, "I'll sort this," and then he is walking away. I swear that he disappears into midair. I try to follow him, but the water is around my feet, and I cannot move.

*

In this life, I go to a party, where I meet my wonderful husband. And now, years later, here I am at the park with our kids. I try not to get weepy, but I'm always weepy. The baby is still strapped to my front as I keenly push Hazel on the swings. Other mums coo at how big she is, how tall she is getting. Yesterday, she won a spelling bee at school.

"C-A-R-O-U-S-E-L," she sings as she hits each fence post with a stick as we walk home. I bump the baby in time.

"C-A-R-O-U-S-E-L," I say too.

We get home.

"How are my girls?" says my husband, tousling the children's hair.

"Daddy!" Hazel laughs.

"What?" he asks.

"Isaac is a boy!"

I wake up in the night and my husband is gone. I creep to the window and can see him walking towards something. I cup my hands around my eyes to try and look through the window, but all I can see is something dark and rippling.

I rush down the stairs, tiptoeing past the children. It strikes me that I can't remember if we have any. I try to sneak up on him, but I trip and he turns around and—

*

I go to a party and I meet this kind and funny and generous man. How long have we been together? Sometimes, if I close my eyes, it feels like forever. Like I can't remember life before marriage and kids and a house and a dog.

I open the children's bedroom door to kiss them goodnight. There's an awful tearing sound, like fabric being ripped into two and suddenly, I am looking through dark holes in the room that lead nowhere. It smells like spilled beer and popcorn and there's a man in the garden and I try to go home but I can't find my bicycle. I go upstairs to the pile of coats on the bed, and I fall asleep next to a girl whose face I can't make out and I —

*

In this life, I go to a party, where I meet my husband and all the dominoes have fallen in a perfect line leading us to this: our first family holiday. We are going to Disneyland. We wake the children in the night with new suitcases and drive to the airport. They are wired with excitement and it is all too much and one of them cries and I ask my husband to pull over so I can comfort them.

"There's no point," he says, eyes fixed on the road.

I feel scared all of a sudden. I close my eyes and remind myself that I know I am lucky. I know I am lucky; I know I am. I'm just tired. I always feel tired.

But then, they don't eat the toast at the hotel breakfast because it doesn't taste like it does at home. One of them slams the bathroom door and it breaks my toe. I feel pathetic and try to call my mum and she tells me to just come home but the phone line cuts her off. I come into the hotel room and my husband has made the bed and bought flowers for me and I smile, but I know he won't be satisfied because it isn't perfect, it's not what he wants.

*

In this life, I am making sandwiches for packed lunches and the knife falls out my hand. Something rips in front of my eyes and our dog Max licks the butter off the knife before becoming a cat, then shifting back, his claws sinking in and out of his paws, his face shifting between golden and black fur. One eye stays the same shape as a cat's: round with a dark slash of a pupil.

I can't find my husband, but my children run down the stairs crying and their faces flicker before me. They are Isaac and Hazel and Laura and a hundred other children I cannot remember the names of.

Children who were born and ones that weren't. They look like me, then him, then me, then both of us, then nothing. Where their faces are supposed to be are just holes and I look at them so long I feel myself being drawn in and I walk closer and closer, not even conscious of moving my feet and I—

*

I wake up and I am making a packed lunch. I take knife a from the block and put it in my pocket. The cat licks butter from the knife, but I pack his sandwich anyway. It's starting to bleed through now - my hands multiply in front of me. I've held this knife before in hands that weren't quite mine.

I pretend to sleep but I don't. When I creep up on him, he still hears me but this time, I have the knife, and I stop him from going wherever he goes to change us. I stop him the only way I can. I stop him from ever going back to the party where we met.

He cries as he bleeds.

"You were such a good wife," he says. He dies believing it.

Perhaps I was stupid or impulsive. I should have found out more about what he did and how. He is lying on our kitchen floor, his blood spilling further and further but I still hesitate, worried I will open my eyes, and it will start again.

I try to sleep, like this is just a dream. I wake up and the house is empty. I lock the front door as I walk away. When I turn back around it is being sucked into the darkness. I know I'll follow soon enough.

Tian Yi

Extract from *The Good Son*

The first time I saw what Owen Li could do, it happened at school.

We must have been eight or nine, an age when I still considered him one of my best friends. We didn't always spend break times together, but that day it was just the two of us kicking an old football around, out of sight in an area of the playground between two buildings. We were asking each other stupid questions, as usual.

What would you rather have, a pet snake or a pet tarantula?

If you could have any superpower, what would you pick?

Would you eat the world's spiciest chilli if I gave you ten quid? A hundred?

We were laughing about something when a boy called Jonny rounded the corner and spotted us. He was in our class, scrawny, but tall. He was always swearing at teachers and being sent home.

Oh look, he said. *Eddie and Owen, sitting in a tree.*

We ignored him like we were supposed to, but Owen Li couldn't quite hide his expression of panic, or the flush that crept over his face. He'd always been quieter and shyer than me. I kicked the football against the wall, but Jonny kept going.

Are you twins or something? Siamese twins, yeah? And then, nonsensically, *Cos I've seen your mums and they're fat.*

I moved towards him before I'd really decided to. I don't think I wanted to hurt him, only to shut him up. My fist, when it connected with Jonny's nose, made a sound like I'd thrown an apple against a hard surface. The sound and the immediate pain in my hand surprised me. I'd never hit anyone before.

For a moment Jonny and I both froze. Then he clutched at his face and bright blood dripped between his fingers onto the faded hopscotch where he stood. He started to make a noise, something strained, but Owen Li was there before he could cry out.

He grasped Jonny's head with both hands and examined him, not at all like a child dealing with another hurt child, but as if he were much older. Watching him, I thought of a vet or a farmer with a wounded animal in his care. What happened next was strange – with one hand, quickly and precisely, Owen Li tapped Jonny on one side of his head, just by his ear. Then he spoke.

It was an accident. I kicked the ball and it hit you. Ed wasn't here. OK?

Jonny seemed to relax, his face becoming oddly blank beneath the shine of blood that coated his mouth and chin. He allowed Owen to walk him towards the school building. A few paces away, Owen turned around, stared at me and put a finger to his lips.

Owen Li and I grew up in the same block of ex-council flats near the centre of town. He lived on the ground floor and I lived on the fourth. A few other Chinese families were nearby and our parents played cards on the weekends, usually at Owen's. There were five of us boys, all around the same age, and we would scurry out to the park across the road, reappearing at dinner time with grazed knees and grass in our hair. We'd pull faces at each other over the lingering smell of cigarettes and the piles of sunflower seed husks on the table.

Our place next time, my dad often shouted as the families dispersed. Owen's dad Lao Li would smile and agree politely. I only realised years later that everyone must have preferred their bigger, tidier flat, where the wallpaper was fresh, not peeling like ours, and where the doors opened out onto a patio, decorated by Mrs Li with fresh flowers, instead of our tiny balcony enclosed by chicken wire.

I used to run down to theirs all the time and not notice the difference. Owen Li was my first real friend, more so than Yong, or Pete, or Haohao, simply because of our proximity. Considering how much time we spent together, I have a clearer impression of the cartoons we watched after school and the crisps and biscuits we ate, dropping crumbs on his squeaky leather sofa, than of any conversations we had.

Of course, I now wonder if everyone recalls their childhood friendships through such a haze, or if there is another reason for my poor memory.

After that day with Jonny in the playground, I went with Owen Li back to his place, as usual. I was sure that Jonny would tell someone about the punch and I would get into trouble. I wanted to ask Owen about it. How had Jonny become so calm? Why had he listened to him so easily? But I didn't say anything. I didn't know if my questions made any sense.

Lao Li joined us on the sofa, throwing peanuts in the air and catching them in his mouth. He and Owen Li had the same narrow shoulders, though Owen had a different way of holding himself – with a sort of tension, instead of his father's ease.

Watching TV again? Don't they give you any homework? Lao Li spoke Mandarin with a thick southern accent and it always took me a few seconds to take in what he was saying. He patted me on the arm while I frowned.

Working hard is what makes a nan zi han, he said. The phrase he used was new to me, but I shook my head confidently as if I understood.

We're not nan zi han, I said. *We're kids.*

That amused him. He laughed so hard I could see the bits of half-chewed peanuts on his tongue.

Of course, he said. *Anyway, you have to know some women before you get to be real men, right?*

I opened my mouth and shut it again when I caught Owen Li watching us. The expression on his face might have been jealousy. Lao Li never really had conversations with Owen, he only snapped or issued instructions. I felt bad about that.

After that day, it seemed like Owen Li started avoiding me, but we might have been growing apart anyway. He was always at some sports or music club, or in extra classes with a tutor, even at weekends. When I turned up at their door, Mrs Li would frown at me, stern and suspicious behind her thick-rimmed glasses, as if I shouldn't have so much free time myself.

The card games with the other families also stopped as we approached the end of primary school. Our parents kept talking about which of us would pass the exams to get into the posh high school in town, where they wore jackets and ties, and I suppose those stakes weren't as fun for them. In the end only Owen Li proved clever enough for St Phillip's. The rest of us were never allowed to forget it.

Be more like Owen! Owen zhen guai! We imitated our parents, nasally, when we all gathered for the occasional Chinese New Year or Mid-Autumn Festival party. It made Owen Li blush, but he put up with it and let us insult him as much as we wanted.

I knew the other boys behaved worse towards him sometimes, especially Pete, who tended to shove him harder than was necessary and laugh with too much of a sneer when Owen was red and speechless. I decided I never would. I had a sense of owing him something for that day with Jonny, even though I told myself there were plenty of reasons for Jonny not to snitch and that I must have imagined anything odd. I kept dwelling on the way Owen Li had spoken to Jonny, with an assurance I'd never seen from him before and the way Jonny's face had changed. I couldn't quite forget it.

We stopped giving Owen Li a hard time about private school eventually, but our parents kept at it. *Such a good boy,* they continued. *Top set in all his subjects! Look, he's got a Saturday job! Nobody needs to worry about him.* They said things like that more often and loudly, when Mrs Li was promoted to head of department at her job and when their family left the flats for a house in the suburbs with a long, landscaped garden.

Children's and
Young Adult Fiction

Noga Applebaum

Extract from *Yearn*

I wake up with a start, my heart is pounding. The sheet under me is wet, my loose fitting *gatches* now sticking to my inner thighs. I keep my head on the pillow and my eyes closed. I hear Aron and Shloime stirring; it must be nearly morning. Soon the Waker on duty is going to bang on our door, calling us to daven *Shachris* and you can't be late for prayers. Not at *Lev Shalem Yeshive* and especially if your father is the Head.

I used to have 'accidents' when I was six or seven and I would tear off the bedding and leave it for *Mame* by the washing machine. She never said a word about it, but there was always a clean sheet in the drawer under my bed. I'm seventeen now and this is just an old memory, yet it is the third time in two weeks that I wake up wet and I don't understand what's happening. Perhaps I've been struck by something, as punishment for all these dreams I've been having. I shiver, but stay put. I have to wait until they go.

The dreaded knock comes.

"Get up! It is time to worship your creator!"

I hear Aron yawn. Soon he is moving round the tiny room gathering his clothes. Shloime always takes longer, he likes to savour the last few minutes in the warm bed but, before long, he too is up and about.

"Rise and shine Yanke!" Aron bellows.

"Will you keep it down *sheygetz*? Nobody wants to wake up to your ruckus," says Shloime. Then, softly, to me: "Come on Reb Kenigson, you'll be late."

"You go ahead, I'll catch up," I say, feigning grogginess.

Aron and Shloime leave without another word. Idle chatting before the Morning Prayer is frowned upon. The Holy One, blessed be he, should always come first.

Once they're gone, I make sure my *kapel* is still on my head and hurriedly drag the plastic bowl from under my bed, spill water on each hand three times with the two handled jug, mumble the blessing and hop up, pulling the cover to hide the wet patch. It should dry by the time I return tonight. As for my *gatches*, I'll have to wear them. I already washed my things yesterday and I can't be seen doing the laundry twice in one week.

It doesn't take me long to dress. I pull the trousers over my damp undergarment, button my white shirt right on left and slip back my sleep-crumpled *tzitzis* over my head, comforted by its familiar fringes hanging by my sides. I stuff my arms into the black sleeves of the *rekel* and grab my hat from the hanger by the door. There is nobody in the corridor, which means that I am seriously late.

The grey morning light skulks around the edges of the courtyard, beyond the reach of the main building's shadow. A group of young men shake their curled *peos*, sprinkling water droplets into the misty air, their faces, still damp, are shiny under their black hats. One of them is humming a melodious tune from the morning prayer, preparing his mind and soul to approach his Maker. I walk fast against the flow, my eyes lowered, the gravel crunching under my feet. I skirt the side of the building until I reach the rusty door set discreetly in the ancient wall. Beyond here, it's nature's territory. Unkempt lawns, overgrown with weeds and brambles, stretch to the edges of a dense copse. No one is supposed to venture beyond this boundary, but tell-tales of crushed undergrowth suggest that not all abide by the rules.

The door is slightly ajar. I squeeze through and descend the stone steps with care. Even though they are fitted with anti-slip strips, the constant moisture means that breaking an arm is still a distinct possibility. My fingers trace the cold and wet wall as I go down. Apart from my footsteps, all is silent. I must be the very last one.

The drab changing area is empty. I hang my hat on one of the pegs, the long *rekel* on another. The *mikveh* is built into the basement, which used to be the servants' quarters before the *Yeshive* bought the place. There is very little natural light filtering through the opaque narrow windows set high in the wall, but bright fluorescents more than make up for it. I undress quickly, the *gatches* are almost dry from the warmth of my body, a blessing, but I still make sure to hide them at the bottom of the pile. I eye the showers. I'm already late as it is, so I decide to skip this part and go straight to the immersion pool. There's no one here to see anyway and if it is unbecoming to be late for *Shachris*, it is even more so for the first lesson of the day.

As my bare feet squelch across the plastic mats that cover the floor, I savour the moment. Usually this room is bustling – boys peeling off their layers, then huddling in the queue, awaiting their turn in the water, averting their gaze from each other's pale flesh. If none of the Authorities are around, there is chatter about community news, or idle gossip is passed around in hushed whispers. Being alone is a rare treat. I walk through the opening that leads to the immersion pools. There are three of them, separated by walls, a set of sunken steps leading down into each. Out of habit I choose the furthest one, but as I'm about to descend the steps, a figure rises from the water, hands reaching up to wipe his eyes and forehead. I lower my gaze, but an image remains on my retina – the flames encircling his face. His short hair, *peos* and slight beard are all red. Not pale carrot but darker and more vibrant. I've never seen this kind of colour before. I've never seen him before. I retreat and hurry down the steps of the middle pool. The water is murky green and reaches to my chest. The smell of chlorine is strong. I take a lungful of air and sink in. Under the water I open my eyes. On the wall opposite me I can see the little hole through which rainwater seeps in from the adjacent container and I imagine these holy drops weaving their way towards me, washing away my vices and purifying every inch of my body. As my breath dwindles, I surface and then plunge in twice more. I climb out of the water, *peos* dripping, arms swishing, the *brith* slap-slapping against my wet thighs as I make my way back to the changing area. The red-headed *bucher* is standing there in his *gatches*, rubbing his hair with a towel. I quickly move towards the bench, keeping my eyes on the cracked wall tiles.

"*Shulem alichem,*" he says pleasantly.

"*Alichem shulem,*" I mumble back, hurrying to my own pile of clothes. I reach out and then realise that in my haste I forgot my towel.

I glance left and right to see if someone's forgotten towel will deliver me, but the bench and the pegs are bare.

"Have mine, I'm done with it," I hear him say and a second later a towel lands at my feet. I pick it up with flushed cheeks and stutter my thanks. A quick rub and I send it back to its owner.

We dress silently. He finishes first and, grabbing his hat, heads out. I look up and he glances sideways. Our eyes meet for a fraction of a second. He smiles briefly, nods and is gone, his footsteps fading up the stairs. I don't have time to dwell on who he is or where he came from. I slip my foot into the right shoe, then the left, then tie the laces, first left, then right. Crushing my hat over my still damp hair, I follow him out.

When I get to the courtyard there is already no sign of him.

Louise Conniss

Extract from *Florence Havelock and the Forces of Nature*

Florence stood at the door of Hawthorn House and pulled the bell for a third time. Why wouldn't someone answer? She stepped back and glared at the house, as if it would offer her an explanation. But the windows were dull and lifeless and the door remained tightly shut.

Swollen grey clouds darkened the autumn sky, while fat raindrops dappled the garden path. *Could this be the wrong house?* Panic flushed through Florence's chest like icy water. She shivered and folded her arms, tempted to go home. There was plenty of work at the factory, but her mother wouldn't hear of it. Not after what happened to her brother.

Florence waited a few minutes more. The rain fell hard. Soon, the road by the house was a torrent of mud and steaming horse manure. Losing patience, she scrunched up her wet skirts and squelched unsteadily over the lawn, towards a window with iron bars. She peered into a gloomy drawing room crammed with ornaments and overstuffed furniture. There was no sign of life.

Before Florence could try the bell again, muffled shouting drifted through the front door. There was a series of clicks and snaps and the door swung open. Out stormed a girl, a couple of years younger than Florence. She was wearing a maid's uniform. An old man stepped out after her. He had white wispy hair like a dandelion clock and dark owlish eyes.

"Millicent please do stay, I promise you she's harmless," he pleaded.

"Harmless?!" shrieked Millicent. "She nearly gave me a heart attack. I'll not step foot in this house again!" Turning on her heels, Millicent knocked Florence sideways as she charged past. Stopping suddenly, she turned to Florence. "I'd stay away from that house if I were you!" She made the sign of a cross, then bolted off down the street as fast as her legs could carry her.

Lost for words, Florence gawked at the old man. His cheeks reddened.

"Ah the new maid!" he wheezed. "Florence, is it? I'm the butler. I suppose you should call me Mr Galanthus. I had expected you at the servants' entrance."

"Oh sorry. Nobody told me to use the servants' entrance," mumbled Florence.

"Don't say another word." He waved Florence into the house. "It's not a mistake you'll make again."

Florence wondered if she should make a run for it herself. But her mother's reaction would be more terrifying than whatever had scared that Millicent girl. Reluctantly, she stepped out of the rain and into a windowless hallway. The air was quiet and still.

"Blimey, it's dark in here!" She didn't like the dark. It was a good hiding place, especially for rats.

"I don't really notice it," said Mr Galanthus. "Let me light some lamps. Follow me." He moved down the hallway, lighting a row of ornate lamps mounted on the wall. Florence could smell the gas before it ignited. At home they could only afford candlelight.

Florence glanced around the illuminated hallway. A lush black and red patterned rug covered the parquet floor, running all the way up to a long staircase at the end of the hall. The walls were covered with plain green wallpaper. As they reached an iron fireplace with a mirrored over-mantel, Mr Galanthus paused to retrieve a white cloth from the floor, and hurriedly draped it over the mirror. Florence could barely look at it. Somebody must have died inside the house recently. The mirrors would have been covered to stop their spirit from being trapped behind the glass.

"The former lady of the house – Clio Hawthorn. A terrible fall down the stairs," sighed Mr Galanthus. "She was Mr Hawthorn's aunt."

A familiar sadness stirred in Florence's chest. She dug her nails into her hands and tried not to cry. "I'm sorry for your loss," she managed to say.

Mr Galanthus nodded. "Anyhow, Mr Hawthorn is expecting you, but he has a visitor right now. We'll wait in the kitchen. You need to dry out before he catches sight of you."

Mr Galanthus lit an oil lamp and led Florence through a door at the end of the hallway and down a dark narrow staircase. *So, there was no gaslight for the servants.* The lamp light cast long shadows as they made their way down the stairs.

Florence gasped as they entered the kitchen. It was bigger than the room she shared with her family. The floor was flagged with stone, and the walls all around were covered with white tiles. An oil burning lamp hung lifeless from the ceiling, and weak grey light leached in through the windows. Embers glowed gently in a large fireplace. Mr Galanthus shovelled on some coal and coaxed the fire back to life with a brass poker.

Above the fireplace was a wooden shelf, or a clavey as Florence's mother would call it. On the clavey sat two strange dolls. A man and a woman. Their heads looked like small wrinkly parsnips with a wig on top and roots sprouted out of their chins like whiskers. Their clothes were made of tatty brown muslin and they wore wooden clogs on their feet. They were slumped against each other as if asleep, the woman's head resting on the man's shoulder. Mr Galanthus followed Florence's gaze.

"That's Mr and Mrs Hobthrush. Much loved by the late Mrs Hawthorn. Been with her since she was a tiny lass."

"Lovely," said Florence. She wrinkled her nose as soon as Mr Galanthus returned to stoking the fire.

"Right, you sit by the fire, though I doubt it'll make much difference." Mr Galanthus frowned.

Florence looked at her dress, still dripping wet from the rain. She gathered up her skirts and gave them a twist. Water poured onto the floor. She stood guiltily in the puddle, like a badly behaved kitten.

Mr Galanthus laughed and ushered her to a wooden chair by the fire.

"We'll clean that up in no time."

When he had finished, he shuffled over to the stove and heated a pan full of milk. "Some cocoa will warm your bones for you."

Florence watched as Mr Galanthus stirred the brown powder into mugs of steaming milk, adding some honey for sweetness. He handed

Florence a mug and a plate of bread smeared with butter and jam, luxuries she rarely tasted at home.

Mr Galanthus settled into an armchair and tucked into his bread. His hands trembled slightly. Florence sipped her cocoa and felt the sweet brown liquid warm her hands and belly. She took a greedy bite of bread and closed her eyes, savouring the creamy sweetness of the butter and jam. It all seemed too good to be true.

Mr Galanthus chuckled. "There's plenty more where that came from – if you stay that is."

"Why wouldn't I stay?" Florence thought about the runaway maid. An uneasy feeling rose from the pit of her stomach.

"Ah, no reason." Mr Galanthus shifted in his seat. "It's... er... just a bit tricky finding staff these days."

"Are there other maids here? I can't clean the house on my own," said Florence.

"No. Just Mrs Wringer, the Housekeeper. But you'll be fine. I'd watch your step though – she doesn't think we need any more help. So, make yourself useful."

"Was the other maid scared of her? Is that why she ran away?" Florence's eyes flitted to the servant's entrance. She hoped it wasn't locked.

"Certainly not! Poor Millicent... she was homesick... desperate for an excuse to leave." Mr Galanthus glanced around the room as he spoke, careful not to look Florence in the eye.

Before Florence could find out more, a brass bell next to the door rang.

"That's coming from the study. Mr Hawthorn must be ready for you."

Mr Galanthus heaved himself up with a grunt and placed the empty pots in the sink.

"Right, follow me."

As Florence stood, she noticed the dolls above the fireplace were sat up straight, their eyes trained in her direction. *How peculiar. Mr Galanthus must have moved them.* She brushed down her skirts and headed up the staircase to meet Mr Hawthorn.

W Y Dobson

Extract from *Firenzo, Realm of Lost Memories*

*T*here was nowhere left for him to go. Below was a sheer drop. If he wasn't gored by rocks, the raging water would swallow him.

Jonty regretted his choices. It had all been a bad idea. Right from the start. If only he hadn't been so careless with Gramps's memoirs, knocking over that *suzu* bell. He wouldn't have met Koku. He wouldn't have drunk that green tea. He wouldn't have walked through the Gate of Memory. And, not least, he never would have met the grandly named Lafcadio - the kappa water imp whose lilting Irish voice he now heard.

"Looks like you're in quite a fix, JoJo. Now do you wish you could have swapped names with me?" shouted Lafcadio from the clifftop's safety. "It's not so bad having a soup dish on your head, not when it's raining witches." He laughed.

"Don't be mean. It's not big of you to scoff," said Mammy Teeth.

"How many times, Mammy! Will ya stop your nippin'!" shrieked Lafcadio.

Squinting, Jonty looked up, bullets of rain hitting his eyes. Mammy Teeth was fully extended from Lafcadio's carapace, her tongue sticking out, that single reptilian eye on its tip fastening its gaze on him. Then the tongue rolled back inside the teeth and she repeated what she had first said to him.

"Choose a way and go down it like a thunderbolt."

In the whole time he had spent in Kamizen, the wisest advice he'd received was from a set of disembodied teeth.

Choose a way. Go down it like a thunderbolt.

And so he jumped.

一 (Tale 1)

申 (Hour of the Monkey)

"Gramps has blown his whistle," Jonty shouted through to the garden and waited for his mother's reply.

Only birdsong and the distant puttering of a lawnmower responded. His mother, Mayumi-Jane, had a lot on her plate. She was also notoriously hard to distract. The garden was her sanctuary, she liked to say, which implied she was escaping from somewhere, and that somewhere right now was Gramps's house where they had moved for the summer. She taught insect evolution at a university and would happily admire butterflies until nightfall.

Jonty reached over Gramps's walking frame parked outside the loo and tapped on the door.

"She's coming," he reassured him.

"No bother," croaked the gentlest of voices.

Jonty stepped outside into the late afternoon glow.

"Mum? Gramps needs you," he said more firmly.

"I heard," said his mother irritably, rising from behind a turret of pampas grass. She grumbled about her knees, walking stiffly towards the house, sunlight catching the magnifying glass in her hand. She mussed Jonty's toasted barley hair. "You look like a Yeti! Read your book at the barber's. Or take a break and kick a football or something, even petty vandalism. Honestly, I despair."

"Yeti hair is all the rage, Mum." Jonty failed to make her smile. While wriggling on a pair of vinyl gloves, she steeled herself, shoving the walking frame out of the way; two rubber chimps abseiling from its crossbar swung wildly as a result. Four summers ago, when Jonty was eight, he had covered the walking frame in jungle-patterned tape to make it more appealing.

Jonty retreated through the kitchen, leaving his mother with Gramps.

"You just went. Have you done another Winslow?" he heard her complain. Soon, the frustrated yelling might begin, which, whenever it happened, made Jonty want to cover his ears and hide.

He was the worrying sort and, seeing her distressed, grouchy and fairly forgetful, sharpened his worries. She worked into the slender hours of the night, while also looking after Gramps. The nursing care company, which sent home help, had gone out of business; apparently there were no alternatives in the whole of South Yorkshire. Mayumi-Jane had no choice but to relocate from Cambridge, taking Jonty with her.

Gramps had pleaded not to be put in a care home. At least not until he could no longer recognise family. For a long time Baba had cared for him and caring for him had taken its toll. A couple of years ago, after a short illness, she had passed away, exhausted.

Now Jonty entered the study. The room was a shrine to learning and art. Books from floor to ceiling and framed artwork from *The New Yorker* magazine filled every inch of remaining wall space. Pride of place, however, was devoted to a blown-up photograph of Doctor Yuri the Chimp, a stethoscope around her neck and smile broader than the East Sea. She had been Gramps's favourite research partner during his work as a primatologist in Japan. Snow monkeys, chimps and their smaller cousin, the bonobo, were his speciality. How Jonty now missed Gramps telling him stories. Stories about trekking after the calls of bonobos in the Congo Basin. Tramping through a rainforest with one shoe, the other lost to the mouth of a crocodile. Wrangling snow monkeys from the bamboo forests of Arashiyama and transporting them to the mesquite brushland of Texas. The thought that those days were now behind them nested a sad chill in his chest. Jonty loved his Gramps. He hated seeing him struggle.

Swivelling on an armchair, he turned his mind to the list pinned to a corkboard above the campaign desk. Lines crossed out three of the ten items. Gramps's memoirs were unfinished and, until completed, he could never settle.

"He's so agitated," Mayumi-Jane had said to Jonty's father on a video call. "He keeps saying, 'My spirit will be restless, I have to finish it.' I've spent months, months knocking it into shape and he's obsessed with the fine details. He can't be expected to remember now – the publisher's being unreasonable."

Jonty's father had listened calmly, nodding sympathetically. "He was a career scientist, who found spirituality in old age. He's questioning his life's work. Sounds like finishing his memoirs means he gets to leave this world in peace. What about the advance – has the publisher asked for it back?"

Jonty hadn't known what an advance was, but figured it involved money. Most things in life involved money. On the call, Mayumi-Jane shrugged off the question, murmuring that it had been spent on carers.

David Lowe

Extract from *Word Thief*

H ush wanted bread.
A familiar ache gnawed at her belly. Hunger was a constant
companion for anyone living rough in the Beneath.

"Out the way!" A merchant barged past and Hush leapt back to
avoid being trampled on. She hated crowds. Too noisy, unpredictable,
full of pointed elbows and harsh words. Still, she wanted bread and
this was undoubtedly the best place to find it.

Grand Market Square was the heartbeat of trade in the Beneath.
In truth, it wasn't really a square, and there was certainly very little
that was grand about it. It was the part of the city where the streets
widened just enough to allow traders to pile in with their wagons
and wares. They did this with little regard for personal space, every
inch fiercely contested, as butchers, blacksmiths, tailors and tricksters
haggled over anything and everything.

Hush tightened her belt around the robes that hung from her
frame. She didn't mind her drab attire; her clothes helped her blend in
and avoid unnecessary attention. People tried to talk to you if you were
noticed and she certainly didn't need that. She'd already spotted one
Bluehead patrol, the ominous glint of steel at their waists marking them
just as surely as the cerulean plumes that jutted from their halfhelms.

She padded around the edge of the street, scanning the crowd
for potential threats while trying to remain hidden. There was
little to remark about her appearance. Her dark hair was kept
short, hacked shoulder length with a blunt knife she'd found. Her
features were pointed and sharp, her eyes the colour of mud. She
had the pale complexion of most Beneathers, a by-product of living
in perpetual gloom, forever in the shadow of the city overhead.

She scowled upwards. The Above rose from the centre of the
Beneath like a colossal sundial. The upper city defied all logic and

reason. Balanced on a pronged tower seven hundred feet in the air, it was home to the wealthy aristocracy who could afford the eye-wateringly expensive real estate. It was a place of money, magic and even fresh air. Or so she'd heard. She'd never be allowed to visit, of course. And her lungs were so used to the soot-blackened smog down here that she probably wouldn't notice the difference in air quality.

A waft of baked bread caught on a sudden gust, bringing her back to the market with a stomach-churning crash. She could see them now, trays of crusty rolls piled high upon a stall. Steam trailed up like a smoke signal. Her pulse quickened and she took a step forward.

"Spare a coin for an old man?" A beggar shook out a hopeful cup, mismatched eyes flashing at Hush from a web of wrinkled flesh.

She swerved out of his reach. If he wanted food, he could get his own. Life was hard enough without helping others.

She refocused on her target, sliding unnoticed through the crowd, until she was a few paces away. The aroma made her light-headed and she wiped away a line of drool that was forming at her lower lip.

She couldn't help herself. Drawn forward like a moth to flame, she stretched out a fingertip to touch a doughy crust. Heat puffed out as the glaze cracked upon contact. Her stomach lurched in anticipation. She could practically taste it. One. More. Inch.

"Get your filthy hands off my stock!"

A hand seized her wrist, twisting her savagely. Hush stared up at a barrel-chested man. He wore a stained apron and his forearms were pockmarked with oven burns. His thick moustache trembled as he hissed through clenched teeth.

"A weevil? In my bread?"

Hush shrank back as panic threatened to overwhelm her. The baker snarled, his fingers a vice about her wrist.

"Well? Got nothing to say? Let's see what the Blueheads think of this, *thief*."

Hush watched in horror as he threw back his head to bellow for the guards.

Fear pooled up from the base of her spine. What would the Blueheads do to her? Beat her? Maim her? Slit her throat and throw her body in the river? One less thieving urchin to cause a nuisance. The unfairness of it all threatened to overwhelm her. Tears stung her eyes, and she felt a lump in her throat. Still, she'd be damned if she let them take her this easily.

Without realising why, without even feeling her mouth move, she spoke a single word, a word that rose unbidden to her lips.

"*Silence*," she whispered.

A cold thrill sent her skin to gooseflesh, her voice both a thousand miles away and reverberating throughout her skull. Her heartbeat thundered, and the air around her seemed to pulse, a single shudder of anticipation.

The baker's brow furrowed and he clutched at his throat with his free hand. For although he'd tried to shout for aid, his face contorting, his jaw tensing, his tongue spraying spittle all over Hush, not a single sound had come from his mouth.

He attempted to cry out again and once more was rendered completely mute, while the hum and chatter of market noise continued around them. Hush had no idea what was wrong with him. It was as though he was in a bubble, through which no sound could pass.

This was her only chance. She lunged into the front of his apron, pulling out a fistful of flour that she flung at his face. He reeled backwards as the white powder exploded on impact, and her free elbow made sharp contact with his groin. He folded over, releasing Hush and heaving in silent pain.

Hush allowed herself a grim feeling of satisfaction. It would take a lot more than some oafish baker to come between Hush and a good meal. She stepped past and reached out for the roll.

"Time to go I think," a soft voice spoke behind her.

Gloved hands yanked her up, away from the stall. She made a final desperate snatch for the roll, but it slipped from her grasp and fell to the floor. She cried out as the baker, now stumbling around pawing flour from his eyes, trod on it, and mashed it into the cobblestone.

She thrust her head forward, determined to bite the fingers that held her. Her teeth punctured through the glove into something rough and gritty. She spat out splinters. Was she going mad? Were the hands made entirely out of wood?

"Keep still," the voice murmured in her ear, quiet and gravelly. "And don't do that again," it added as an afterthought. "You'll lose a tooth."

She couldn't see her captor. They'd snuck up from behind (the coward) and now she found her back was pressed against their front. She felt a coarse shirt against her spine and although they didn't seem especially large, there was a certain wiry strength that made it impossible to break free.

Her vision wobbled as she was carried into the crowd. Dimly she became aware that the baker's cries for help were now audible, but they were soon lost in the madness of the market flaring up around her.

Snarling faces, shrieking animals, hissing oil, the chop and snap of cut meat, the press of bodies and above it all, a swirling surge of braying, burning white-hot noise. All the while those wooden hands held her, locking her into the nightmare.

Hush felt her eyes roll back and everything went dark.

E J Robinson

Extract from *Swordfern*

*T*he turning leaves had just begun to glint with autumn gold when the first child was taken. A boy, spirited away as though by fairies... although fairies were not known to leave the blood of children trailing from cradle to cave. First one child, then one more, then another, snatched from the village of Swordfern as if by magic.

There was talk of tricksters, demons and witchfolk roaming the night, seeking young flesh to appease their devilish appetites. The elders ordered the village gates heaved shut, men mounted the walls armed with fire arrows and the women kept smoking fires lit at every corner of the perimeter, all in hopes to sight and slay the elusive enemy. Still the youngest of their number were taken, somehow, and never seen again. At least, not in one piece. No one in the village saw or heard a thing.

The womenfolk took to gathering the remaining youngsters round their fires at each darkening of day that they might rest safe under watchful eyes. It was these wakeful women who glimpsed it at last.

A wolf.

A beast the like of which had never been seen. Tall as a horse and muscled as oxen, with teeth sharp as spears and its rough hide matted with the blood of their children. It slipped through shadows as though it obeyed no mortal laws, as though it travelled underneath some protecting evil eye. The villagers retreated into their homes. They barred their doors, blocked their windows, and cut themselves off from one another.

So things were when one mother faced a dilemma of the heart.

Her own mother lived alone beyond the village wall, deep within the forest of Swordfern, where she was sick and in dire need of supplies. But every woman had to keep her fire lit and guarded; any villager found in violation of their duties would face grave penalties. She had no choice but to put together a basket of provisions and call her daughter to her. She wrapped the girl in the remains of her dead husband's chainmail, pinned an oatmeal-coloured hooded cape beneath her *dimpled chin and warned her to keep to the path. The girl slung an axe over her shoulder – a gift from the local woodcutter – hung the basket of food and medicine on one elbow and took up a crackling torch.*

The instant the child's boots touched woodland floor, the wolf's stained snout shot skyward. It was a creature of the forest. It knew the wolds and the gullies and the passes and it knew the path that led from the village to the river crossing and the old stone cottage by the lake's edge where three yew saplings stood in a row. Salivating jaws slack, it rose onto all four paws inside a den littered with the bones of innocents and sprang in the direction of the girl's scent.

But, like the big bad wolf, the girl – whose name was Clothilde – was also a creature of the forest. She too had a nose for scent and ears that had spent years catching every sound on every breeze. She paused now by the three yew saplings and strained to listen. Through the rustling leaves she heard claws slash through undergrowth, the wolf closing in, bearing down on her from the north. The girl set down her basket, slipped the axe off her shoulder and gripped it close. When a streak of grey sliced the emerald-tinted sunshine, Clothilde was ready.

In a flash, she drop-rolled across the path so the wolf snapped only air before it crashed into hardened earth with a snarl of fury. As the animal gathered itself to strike again, Clothilde smote a blow to its head with the butt of her axe and, though it went down dazed, she wasted no time. The girl leapt atop the beast, slammed one boot down on its baby-guzzling throat, and wielded the axe above her head.

"I'm badder than you," she said, then swung.

When the wolf lay slain, Clothilde retrieved her basket. She delivered the food and left the axe with her thankful grandmother, then dragged, heaved and pulled the wolf's carcass back to the village where she slung it down in the market square. Clothilde unpinned her hooded oatmeal cape, dipped it in the blood of her kill, then called the villagers from their homes to tell them their enemy was dead. The people gathered wide-eyed to look upon the small girl with the bloodstained hands and crimson bonnet who stood astride their dead foe like a conquering gladiator.

From that day forth she was known as Clothilde De Wulf, though it was not by this name, but by her blood-dipped bonnet that she would be best remembered. Little Red Riding Hood. The baddest girl to ever take a walk through the woods.

The village folk buried the wolf and, in return for her service, built Clothilde and her mother and grandmother a manor house of wood to replace the rickety hut in which they lived.

Clothilde lived on for many years. She grew up and had a daughter of her own, who in turn lived in the manor the villagers had built on the barrow and she had a daughter, who had a daughter and on and on. It came to be said that the forest and the village would stand safely, protected from its enemies forever... as long as a De Wulf daughter guarded Swordfern.

The day before the ritual, Rowan De Wulf rolled over in bed to squint at the clock on her nightstand, then rubbed her grass green eyes in disbelief and looked again. Her bleary vision hadn't deceived her, it was after midday. Groggily, she pushed her pillows aside and sat up. Why hadn't her parents woken her? And why did her head feel like someone had been chipping at her brain with a pickaxe while she slept?

As she sat blinking sleepily in the half-light, Rowan heard snores floating down from the bunkbed above and realised she wasn't the only one who'd slept in. Her twin sister Ash was also an early riser, so it was odd that she too was still asleep, but not as odd as their parents letting them sleep in in the first place.

"MUM? DAD?" Rowan called, then gritted her teeth at the throb in her temple. She hadn't had a headache this bad since the time she'd stood too close to the batter in rounders.

Surprised her shout didn't stir her sister, Rowan decided against stretching up to shake her awake. It was so easy to accidentally trigger Ash's temper that to deliberately do so was lunacy. Instead, she threw back the covers and slid out of bed.

The first-floor landing was as dim as dusk, speared only with needles of sunshine that pierced through the moth-nibbled holes in the closed curtains. It was afternoon, and her parents hadn't yet opened the eyes of Swordfern Manor. With the exception of Ash's soft snores from the bedroom behind her and the throaty *tock-tick* of the old grandmother clock on the ground floor, the house was silent.

"Mum? Dad? Are you up?"

Nothing.

The breeze that ruffled Rowan's hair carried no tempting breakfast aromas of bacon or toast or coffee. She heard no sizzling pans, nor whistling kettle, no muffled back and forth of parental chatter or far-away rustle of newspapers from the kitchen. The scents and sounds of a normal morning were weirdly absent, but weirdest of all were the ghosts. Rowan padded the length of the landing without seeing a single one.

Stacey Taylor

Extract from *Making Waves*

T he ship is getting closer and I'm ready to lure it to its doom with the power of my voice.

I've waited fourteen years to be able to sing across the turquoise waves and now everyone I know is here to witness this special event and to listen to a voice so beautiful it could only belong to a siren.

I move myself into position on the rock, ignoring the other sirens in my line of sight. When I start to sing, they will join in, creating the most bewitching sound imaginable.

My sister Anya won't be singing, though. She's extremely annoyed that I turned fourteen first and she doesn't have her singing voice yet. I can feel her shooting evil looks at me from her rock, but I do my best to ignore her. She is not going to spoil my big day.

Rays of sunlight dance on the calm water and I know that even the sun is holding its fiery breath, waiting for the inevitable, watching a siren come into her own.

I focus my attention on the large ship as its sails billow in the ocean breeze. It's time to start shifting into human-form, our tails disappearing – a great trick to make sailors feel more at ease. I don't feel too guilty though because how silly do you have to be to see some random women singing on rocks in the middle of the ocean and think, *I know, I'll just sail over and say hi?* It's their own fault.

Anyway, I'm ready. This is my moment and I'm going to give it my all. Closing my eyes, I take a deep breath and start to sing. And that's when everything starts to go wrong.

"Noooooooooooooo," calls my Aunt Pearl as my eyes fling open in surprise. "Stop, stop, stop. Stop now!"

"What's that horrible noise?" yells my Aunt Mayflower. "My ears, my poor ears."

"I don't think I have ears anymore." That was my Aunt Argo, no longer my favourite aunt.

"It's her!" says Anya, looking gleeful and pointing in my direction. "It's Seren. She can't sing."

Horrified faces stare at me from various rocks as a grey cloud moves in front of the sun.

"The ship is changing course," calls one of my cousins. "It's going in the other direction. You've put them off."

This can't be happening; no this is most definitely not happening. I hold my hand against my throat. Am I ill? I don't understand. I'm a siren and I've waited my whole life to do this – this is what I'm meant to do, the whole point of my existence.

There's complete silence now – Anya is still grinning, but trying her best to hide it behind her long hair, which I also think is laughing at me.

My mother was sitting proudly on a rock in the distance, but the rock is now empty. As I look below me into the shimmering water, even the fish have dispersed. I can't even spot any clownfish and they're always everywhere.

I take one final glance at the ship. The bulky structure is moving away faster now, if that's possible and is already close to being a tiny dot on the horizon. Is my voice really that bad? I feel like the sky is closing in on me and the sun has disappeared completely.

I change back to siren form and dive into the waves so suddenly that my tail creates an epic splash in the direction of Anya's rock. I don't stop to enjoy it though; I need to find the rest of my family.

It doesn't take me long to find them in the deep blue water where my mother is being consoled by a group of her siren sisters. The mood is dark. Even the vibrant colours of the anemones do little to help.

"You've brought shame on our family," my mother says when she sees me. "Complete shame." Her dark hair is flowing out behind her and curling at the ends, like it is about to point at me and shout. I'd have preferred it if she'd chosen to go with an 'Are you OK, Seren?

I care deeply about you because I'm your mother,' kind of vibe, but never mind.

"I'm sorry," I say. "I don't know what happened. I did everything I've been taught to do. Please let me try again. Give me another chance."

She looks around at the group and then back at me. "We can't risk it. What if it happens again?"

"Then help me," I say desperately. "I can learn how to sing. I'll improve."

"Your voice is not something you learn," she says. "It's within you."

I don't know what else to say. So that's it then? My voice is my voice?

"We'll tell the others she was unwell," says one of my aunts. "That she shouldn't have attempted to sing today."

There's another long silence.

"You'll keep out of the way for now," says my mother eventually. "Hopefully this will be forgotten soon. *If* we're lucky."

Then she turns from me and so does her hair.

I swim off into the distance, trying my best not to cry. No, I won't cry. I glide through the rotting tangle of an ancient shipwreck which is so old none of the current siren community had anything to do with its demise.

I rest against the sharp, jutting wood as I play back my debut siren-singing moment again and again in my mind, trying to fathom what happened, whilst I'm in the fathoms. Did I do something wrong? Maybe I used the incorrect breathing technique and I didn't sing from the diaphragm like we've been taught?

Or maybe I should have done those weird vocal warm-up exercises that Anya told me to do, making silly faces and silly sounds, though she hasn't made her singing debut yet, so she doesn't know anything. She's never going to let me forget this and I'll never forget the gleeful look on her face as I experienced the worst moment of my life.

I feel uncomfortable and it's not just embarrassment. I feel... what is the word? Unsafe? I mean, I'm not saying my fellow sirens are going to harm me, but they – *we* – don't have a great record when it comes to er... death and destruction.

I know what will calm me down – my grandmother. She is wise and respected and she will influence my mother positively.

She wasn't at my singing debut because she's so important she doesn't travel to events, we just all visit her.

I make my way to her, hoping that news hasn't spread. As I approach her dwellings I can hear whispers. My mother is there. I stay hidden behind coral.

It's OK, she's catching up with her own mum, telling her her troubles – that is a completely normal thing to do and nothing to be alarmed about.

"She will never be a true siren," says my mother. "Without a decent singing voice, she will continue to bring shame on our family."

I wait for my grandmother to impart pearls of wisdom.

"Seren needs to be terminated," she says.

Translation

Margaret Morrison

Extract from *The Turn of the Rope*

Translated from *Tournevire* by Celine Arnauld

Tournevire is an experimental novel by the French/Romanian poet Céline Arnauld, published in Paris in 1919. It is one of the first of very few novels to come out of the Dada movement.

Marinetti wrote of it that "I have read this novel over and over with a profound intellectual pleasure. It is full of blazing suggestive fantasy and virile colour. I read the book in prison, so I know passages off by heart."

Reading the novel today we may well find it quite bewildering and imagine that being in prison might actually have been a great help to Marinetti in appreciating it. The library at the San Vittore Prison in Milan was presumably not well stocked with pot boilers and self-help books.

Tournevire, as a title, is the name of an antiquated piece of nautical equipment like a capstan, that 'turns and turns.' It's a narrative that twists about and goes nowhere. It draws from folklore and fairy tales but, ultimately, is about images and shocking and unexpected words and ideas. Added to the folkloric themes are modern intrusions which remind us that this was published in the immediate aftermath of the trauma of the Great War.

The book consists of six chapters – the final one being a poem competition between the characters, a "lyrical tournament, the prize for which was the knowledge of the future."

It ends inconclusively – because what conclusion can we expect? Dada is not about the neat tidying up of a realist plot. It's about the ride and, in this novel, Arnauld takes us on the start of a madcap Dada ride that can only end in poetry, as it began.

These extracts are from the final chapter.

The Former Artist's Song
Cinema

Carthaginian oxen with their heads ablaze

Were leaping towards the sun

And along the roads whitened villages

Crashed on the burning horizons like breaking waves

I leaned over the dying giraffe

And drunk with vertigo I cursed your gaze

The scimitar buried deep in my chest

I vomited my capsizing life onto the silver screen

And when the capstan's turn brought up the body

I caught you gritting your teeth

The Village Idiot's Song

Farandole

Round and around the Eiffel Tower the wooden horses turn
and the sun at the summit summons the aviator...

I saw your destiny
and I drained delightedly
a glass that once had been
full of fever and of gin...

I bought a book from a bouquiniste
from the pages something fluttered
I saw your name
my name

                    from our past, a letter

At the church square at Mareille
a funeral was held

Gadifer's Song

Magic

The bell tolls
　　　　the world kneels

My foot slipped on the coping of the well
and the water mirror swells around my neck.

They lead the dance at the crossroads
They trample a coffin
You dance in a circle in the mud
The bat hovers over our lives

From the depths of the clear water
the eerie silence
sent the fish towards the harbourside

A wave broke and at your feet it died
On your dress, was that a teardrop
　　　　or the seafoam

I rose slowly toward the sun
only to fall back into your skirmish storm
But I saw the joy in your eyes
　　　　　　and I ran away

A world of scoundrels
　　　　　　was born in the valley

Helena Tebeau

Extract from Growing Southern Plants in the Michurin Method
Translated from *Uprawa roślin południowych metodą Miczurina*
by Weronika Murek

As Maria warmed, her memory thawed. She remembered the hair salon, the beige windows of the front display case, the hairstylist smoking a cigarette on the steps under the sign 'Hair Salon: Masters of Curling'. She remembered the trash bag filled with hair, tightly tied off at the end, wisps protruding from it like the root of an onion. She remembered the woman on the street corner with a tray around her neck, selling batteries of all sizes, stacked side by side like lumps of nougat. She remembered her neighbour returning with his dog from his daily walk, sluggish, staggering, on cue and in rhythm. Maria thought about her last trip to town – her hurried conversation with the woman cleaning the staircase, grabbing her keys and coins slipping from her bag, spinning counterclockwise. And finally, she thought about her last visit to her apartment. She was struck that she remembered it as a visit, as if she had already been a stranger in a place where she no longer belonged, despite the fact that she had been returning home.

But the farther she moved from the hot barrel of the chestnut stove, the less vivid her memories became, as if they were once again sinking into the depths of the boiling, salted water.

From now on, it'll forever be like this, she thought, crossing to the other side of the street, towards the apartment. She peeked into the mailbox – nobody had written. *If what people are saying is true*, she told herself, *then this will continue and I have to accept it: moments will become even more transparent, sliding softly across the rim of the hour. Days and weeks will pass, weighed down by habit and nothing more – that's what it'll be like.*

"Please don't go in there," she heard behind her.

Her apartment door was wide open and with it drifted the scent of lemon detergent.

"This is a place of death. I just cleaned it. Everything is wet."

"Oh," responded Maria, "I'm not entering, I'm just looking."

She broke off.

"This is my apartment. Maybe I can take off my shoes and tip-toe around." She bent down and began to untie her shoelaces.

"Did they call?" the woman asked.

"What?"

She stepped on the heel of her shoe and slid her foot out, kicked it by the wall and bent over again.

"About the disinfection," the woman said.

"No, no one called."

"They probably called, but you don't know. You have to have your affairs in order. I'm going to mop now, so please don't come in, you hear? You have to wait. Or you'll walk in and leave footprints."

"Fine," Maria said, "for a minute here or there."

The woman moved away slowly. Before disappearing behind the bend of the steps, she threw Maria a suspicious look.

So quick, this disinfection, Maria thought, *as if they're covering my traces.*

A sudden bubble of anger seized her. She put on her shoes, tied the laces carefully, and entered the apartment. The drapes and curtains had been taken down; the apartment seemed more spacious than she had remembered it. In the living room the couch was relocated to the wall and plastic bags thrown over it, the wardrobe emptied and books taken off the shelves and moved to the floor.

"So," the woman emerged in the doorway behind her, "you decided to come in, I see footprints."

"Let me be," replied Maria, "It's not the end of the world."

She approached the couch and looked into one of the plastic bags.

"My things. My green dress. Who gave you the right?"

"Disinfection. It all must be disinfected." After a second: "Maybe we should open the window, there'll be a draft, it'll dry faster."

"Disinfection," repeated Maria, "But I lived cleanly."

"The apartment's for sale," the woman replied.

She went to the window, opened one, then the other. In the bright room, she seemed younger to Maria – her face, though wrinkled, was framed by a surprisingly thick and velvety ponytail. She had twisted a thin braid from the centre of her forehead to the nape of her neck, contrasting her shiny forehead like a fresh, unevenly sewn scar.

She reached into her semi-circular pocket, pulled out a slip of paper, folded it a few times, and nimbly propped it under the windowsill.

"It makes no difference if someone lives cleanly. The apartment is for sale and it must be disinfected, business as usual. There are rules."

"But please just look, I'm still alive here."

"Okay," she responded, approaching the plastic bags and tying one off. "That's good. Don't have to explain yourself. You're grown, you did as you pleased. Nothing to be ashamed of."

On the desk, papers were strewn about and Maria began sifting through them. Someone had logged into her inbox, printed her emails, and read through them, leaving snake-like underlines under the intimate fragments. Her diary was open to an entry from March 2000; someone scribbled in pink marker her passwords and social security number.

"Someone hacked into my inbox. They read my diary."

"They probably thought they'd find something worthwhile," she responded, packing books into a box. Following the rhythm of her movements, a strip of light danced across her hair.

Right next to the papers and her diary, a colourful dustpan and a green detergent bottle had been left and Maria, collecting her thoughts, reached for it and pretended to read the label: 'Thanks to us, damp basements and apartments are clean again.'

What a life, she thought with sudden rage, *waking up early each day to braid your hair. To leisurely plait your hair, braiding it so deliberately, and then leading a small life the rest of the day. Leaning over a bucket with your detergents, thanks to which, damp apartments are once again dry. Accepting that no one will ever pay attention to you and, if they do, they will immediately forget about your unexpected, opulent braid; forget about that brief moment wasted in vain. Not having to worry about anything, but getting up in the morning to braid a braid,* Maria thought angrily. *To braid your hair every morning, inspired by diligence, a true female attentiveness that Maria never had. And if Maria had lived identically, perhaps she would not have died and if she had, it wouldn't be now and it wouldn't have been like this, but in a better way, at a more convenient time.*

Footsteps from the stairwell echoed and the floor squeaked: whoever had arrived had stopped in front of the threshold and was now taking off their shoes. After a while, an older man entered the room, carrying a pot wrapped in a towel.

"Dinner," he said, "soup's still warm."

"Good," the woman replied, "the lady from the death is here."

"Because it's my apartment. Because I'm still alive."

"Okay." He set the pot on the table and unwrapped the towel and lifted the lid.

"Everyone read these," Maria pointed to the desk, "didn't they? You both read them?"

"Yeah," replied the woman, "we read them. You hear that, old man, we read them, right?"

"We always read," the man said, "for a laugh."

"But mainly the family does. They're more interested."

"We look through. There isn't much time for that now; you have to search for your glasses, and then you just don't have any energy. But sometimes, to do nothing but work, cleaning these empty apartments, who can stand that? It's for a change of pace." He nodded at Maria, adding, "Have you seen the bed? The dark spot? How am I going to deal with it, what am I going to use to clean it?"

He turned to the woman: "Eat, eat, it will be cold soon."

"What do you mean?" Maria asked. "They said it happened in the bathtub."

"No," the woman replied, "Not in the bathtub. In bed, they were very clear."

"We have guidelines, we work according to them," the man said, walking into the small room. "Some things we separate, some things we give to the poor, some things we burn."

"I'll take it all with me," Maria said, following him.

"I don't know, there are guidelines. Do you see the stain?"

Maria stood by the bed. The sheet and blanket had been removed, only a mattress with a dark, narrow stain resembling a carob pod remained.

"Facing the wall," the woman said from the other room, her mouth full.

"The window," he responded.

"The wall."

"You see this often," he said, "It's unheard of, how often people die."

"But I don't want to," said Maria, taking two steps back. "I don't want to, I don't want to."

Non-fiction

A D Aaba Atach

Extract from *How Dare a Woman*

Tehran, 1999

I t was the day when my father – *Baba* – received an abrupt
phone call informing him that the editorial board for the *Salam*
newspaper would not be meeting until further notice. Though not
a journalist by training, during the short-lived and fast-paced days
of the newspaper, Baba would write regularly about current affairs.
He was in his late 20s, but he was already being described by his
chiefs as a promising up-and-coming force within Iranian politics.
"He has a strong pen," I would later hear frequently from his former
colleagues in Iran, in appreciation of his writing. But, on July 7th, he
knew from the tone of his colleague's voice on the phone that this was
no ordinary cancellation.

Earlier that week, *Salam* newspaper had leaked a government
memorandum that had revealed the Islamic Republic's plans for
the suppression of reformist publications, of which *Salam* was one.
Until then, and for the first time since the inception of the Islamic
Revolution in 1979, the newly elected government, under President
Mohammad Khatami, had given Iranians a taste of what a progressive
– though never quite liberal – Iran could be: no longer wishing death
upon the Americans nor the Brits, but looking ahead toward *dialogue,
democracy, civil society,* or so they said. Khatami had promised many
things, amongst them the protection of press freedoms, so that the
new generation could transcend the muted voices, the whispers and
the stifled expressions of their parents. The age of compliance was
over, to be replaced by a society where your thoughts could be aired,
even published; where women and men could mingle, talk and debate
freely in neighbourhood cafes, to the robust aroma of tobacco and
freshly brewed tea, hands occasionally swaying ever so slightly closer,
close enough for the fingers of the opposite sex to brush against each

other; *freedom*, with all its breeze, yearning, joy. Iranians had been sold a dream and now they wanted to live it.

The memorandum had been written by a former intelligence operative, Saeed Emami, who had been taken into custody over his involvement in a harrowing series of assassinations of opposition figures, which had haunted the nation between 1988 through the waning years of the 1990s. Within days of the leak, the Clerical Court had mandated the swift closure of the newspaper and its publisher, Mohammad Mousavi Khoeniha, had been summoned. Though Baba did not yet grasp the scale of the coming uproar, the day before we were to protest the newspaper's closure, he knelt before me and tried to explain why he might disappear at any moment, just as three of his colleagues already had. I was a month short of turning five, but that was a peripheral matter. In a country where my childhood could be stolen at any moment, he saw no need for sugar-coating. He wanted me to be fully informed, as any adult would be.

He had become a father to a daughter in a country where women held but half the worth of their male counterparts; he was not going to hide this fact. Sometimes, people stopped him on the street, insisting I should be veiled, mistaking me for an older child. There was also a time when the mosque custodian had ordered my father to send me to the women's side because I was a distraction in the men's. He had refused, fierce and unyielding, disturbing the prayers of others. He could have managed the situation better, but this was an exhibition of agency, to demonstrate *for me* that the country's rules were arbitrary and I had to bargain, or fight, my way in. Sometimes it worked, other times it didn't, but that's just how it was. I would go where he went, see what he saw, hear what he heard and, through his access as a man in a deeply patriarchal society, gain my own.

On July 9th, it was no different. Still in touch with his friends at the University of Tehran's Faculty of Law and Political Sciences, Baba met up with some of them in the Islamic Student Association near their Amirabad dormitory and brought me along. I recall it was getting dark and the atmosphere was charged – some wanted to start their protest at night-time. Baba was not at ease and he had not told my mother – *Maman* – of our whereabouts. He couldn't, it was too risky, but he also did not want her to be concerned, not so soon. Though they had separated, they did not see it reasonable to do so with hostility – not yet – so they often remained in communication with each other, for my sake.

That night, Baba relieved himself of duty and we returned to his temporary residence not too far from the dormitories. Baba should have dropped me off at Maman's – after all, the weekdays I belonged with her. She did not know Baba had driven us over 1,000 kilometres to Tehran at a time when he was a wanted man by the government and should have stayed in Urmia, a largely detached and quiet town located in the northwest of Iran.

While Baba tactically planned for a second attempt at protesting the following day, some of his peers already set out to do so when the night was at its darkest. Their efforts, however, were cut brutally short. At 3am that night, while we were sound asleep, over 400 police officers broke into the dormitories, methodically searching each room, not shy to assault any student along the way. By the time Baba and I woke up to his friend's erratic phone call, over 800 student rooms had been ransacked, stomped over, damaged, windows shattered, books thrown out. To Baba's fury and to the shock of his friends and colleagues in Tehran, five of their fellow university members had been killed, 400 wounded, and half of that number arrested. While Maman's concerned phone calls went straight to voicemail, Baba prepared us for a fight. Maman still did not know of our whereabouts or that we were heading to what later became known as Iran's Tiananmen Square moment.

At the university campus, as we joined those mourning in a sit-in protest only hours after the attacks, Baba pressed a strip of duct tape across my lips and then his own, to symbolise the voice that the Iranian public no longer had. Baba told me the campus was the safest place to be, though I am not sure if that was to alleviate my heightened anxiety as a child or if he was naive enough to believe so himself. Baba did not know at the time that with each passing minute the security forces were encircling the campus, soon hoping to block the main entrances and exits. The Deputy Minister for the Interior, also at the protest, was notified first of this and warned the students nearby that the security forces may open fire any minute if the protest were to escalate.

Baba, though mournful and outraged, knew he was responsible for my safety. I'm not sure if he sensed something amiss or if the potential for gunfire spurred him into action, but he removed the duct tape from his mouth to plan a route with his friends that would lead us back to his car. The unending expanse of bodies, as they stood densely packed, made it difficult to find an exit and after much manoeuvring, Baba and I wove our way through the waves of people, exiting from a lesser-known social trail between the faculty buildings. Hand-in-hand, we hurried. I struggled to keep up with his pace. It felt like he knew something I didn't. The simmering heat of the dark grey asphalt seeped through the soles of my shoes as our strides quickened. When I glanced back, the reason for Baba's urgency hit me like a jolt: a dozen police officers in light green uniforms were closing in. They had recognised him and, now, they were coming for us.

Carole Aubrée-Dumont

Extract from *Dumb: A Story About Silence and Resistance*

I t is the autumn after the end of the third and last national lockdown in the UK. I have taken my son Dexter to the hairdresser in Hove and, despite Dexter's fidgeting, they have managed to give him a delightful cut. Having just got on the bus, I realise – too late – that it is full. Aged ten, Dexter still looks like a cherub – especially with his new haircut enhancing his delicate jawline, almost that of a baby. When meeting strangers, he often flashes the most disarming smile, in a way that is different to other children. This makes me feel fiercely protective of him, as well as aware of the passengers' reactions.

No one on board understands that he cannot bear to queue or wait or stand. So, no one moves to let him sit down.

Perhaps it is because I'm French, but I've never been someone who feels comfortable asking for help. I find it difficult; my pride suffers. Right now, instead of doing so, I try to talk quietly to Dexter.

"It's alright, darling – the bus is busy, so we're going to have to stand – stay close to me." My low voice getting lost on the noisy bus, I take hold of him, as well as one of the vertical bars, and hope for the best. But, already palpitating, my heart sinks.

After a few minutes, having lost his balance when the driver applied the brakes, unable to stand unsupported and struggling to tolerate the busy environment, Dexter becomes increasingly agitated. I manage to negotiate a folding seat that has just become free. Just as I am positioning him to sit, an older woman slides into it. Dexter cannot bear nor comprehend this. But, having no language, he is unable to say, "That was my seat!" So instead, he grabs all of my hair and pulls so savagely that I hear it ripping from my scalp. I barely keep myself from howling. His anger has given him enormous strength and his behaviour frightens other passengers, including the seat stealer who, lost for words, stays in her seat. There is no point in trying to disentangle Dexter – this would escalate his behaviour. All

I can do is put my hand on his to reduce the pressure. He pulls and pulls until, in tears, I finally scream across the bus: "Will anyone let my disabled son sit down?"

A young man gives up his seat at the back, but it is too late. *Le mal est fait.* Dexter has been triggered again, this time by my alarming voice. When we reach our stop ten minutes later, he refuses to leave and starts pulling my hair again. I keep my head down to reduce the extent of the pull and to avoid the passengers' stares. Once I have finally managed to get him onto the street by carrying him along the aisle (both of us a mess of tears and shrieks), I realise we are opposite Waitrose and he is going to want to bolt into the supermarket. Having passed what, in our everyday life, I call 'Dexter's threshold', he now needs to explore, expand, exceed his frustration by confronting more crowds, a multitude of food and drink, the buzz of an intensely lit place filled with tempting multicoloured goods. Shuddering, I try to guide him in the opposite direction, towards home. I'm too late to respond, again. In moments of emotional overstimulation, he is drawn to more noise, more lights, more overpowering sensory input, anything that can get him to the edge of feeling. He fights me to get into the store. Seeing us barge in, the guard, who loves having conversations with Dexter through signs and gestures, starts waving at us. But today, enraged Dexter ignores him and darts towards the crisp shelves. Breathless, panicked and self-conscious, I chase him through the aisles. Dexter grabs packs of biscuits and prods a customer's bottom. "Sorry, sorry," I whisper, still racing after my son as he travels, howling, across the store. Not daring to look at the guard, I force Dexter out and guide him along the high street, holding his left shoulder with my left hand, his right hand in mine.

As the two of us arrive back home, my husband stops strumming his guitar in the kitchen, and my daughter pokes her head around her bedroom door. I cannot find the words to explain to them why I am shaking and crying, why Dexter is now throwing the contents of the living room at me. And neither of them wants to make Dexter feel inadequate by rushing to comfort me.

NON-FICTION

Trying to sleep later that evening, I struggle to understand why, when we had got on the bus, to stop the war already threatening to erupt from my son, I wasn't able to announce to the bus passengers in a loud and clear voice that he needed a disabled seat.

The scene is one of many that punctuate my everyday life. I live with my experiences as a mother to Dexter on a constant basis. They are part of a grander scheme of things, that I regularly describe in writing in bureaucratic forms, as well as orally during meetings. Dexter hurling picture frames across the hallway at home; Dexter kicking me in the face from a climbing frame when I asked him to leave the playground; Dexter chucking a pair of scissors across a room filled with children; twice throwing the remote control at the TV and smashing the screen; kicking my pelvis, where he grew, with all his might.

Sometimes, numbed by physical and emotional pain, I remember what a professional once said to me when the challenging behaviour started: "You shouldn't be affected by it." Naive, I felt guilty for not being stronger. As Dexter's mother, I should have been able to cope with whatever he was throwing at me.

It has taken me over ten years to realise the professional was wrong. When a child has no words:

no words to say that they do not agree with a decision;

no words to protest;

no words to assert their point of view;

no words proving that they have a voice, that their opinion matters, that their feelings are valid;

And, when they are denied the prospect of ever being able to express themselves verbally...

They will only be able to use physicality to express frustration. Parents will need specific, effective tools and professional support to help their child out of this prison. If I am not in the room with my son, translating his sounds into actual words so that his interlocutor can understand and reply, there is no possibility that Dexter will be heard.

"EEEee, eee," Dexter might say, scratching his tummy.

"EEEee?" *What is it you're trying to say, my love?*

"Yeeeaaah. EEE."

There is no worse feeling than not being able to understand what your distressed child is attempting to communicate.

After a few minutes, even though I feel out of my depth, by using my intuition alone, I still try: "EEE... Itchy?"

"Yeeeaah!"

Bingo. An itchy tummy. But I am not always able to intuit what Dexter means. Sometimes, I fail and have no choice but to leave him lost for words.

Whilst he doesn't have any interest in the written word, his great receptive skills (his listening – the way he receives language and information, as opposed to the productive or active skills of speaking and writing) mean that he can understand far more than we realise. Didn't he once, only aged three, delicately detach some crumbs from the corner of his slice of cake and hand them to my mum after I casually asked him in French if he might share it (*"tu peux en donner un peu à Mamie, Dex?"*)? It does not feel too far-fetched to believe that my seemingly wordless son is, in his own way, bilingual.

Life with Dexter has been a ride and I can remember every chaotic detail, every silence, every joy and every tragedy. Unlike the silence that couched my family history growing up, I have determined to take the opposite route, in writing down my story.

Yiota Demetriou

Extract from *4757 Miles from Home: A Matrilinear Memoir of Belonging*

Aradippou, Cyprus, 1958

T he corset's steel bones dig into Yiota's flesh with each panicked breath. Aged 14 and trapped, she perches on the edge of a bridal cushion like a sparrow yearning for freedom.

The bedroom door bursts open, a wave of musky perfume engulfing her. Aunties swarm with shrieks and their suffocating hugs reek of expectation. Yiota flinches as they descend. Rouge streaks her cheeks, war paint gone awry. She rubs the smudges, body stiffening as realisation dawns. *Weddings hide thorns among flowers.*

The aunties' eyes narrow, predator-like, as they assess their prey. It's for the *allamata*,[1] she's been told – the ritual marking her passage into womanhood. Her eyes flick to the colourful bonbons on the table. Her hand reaches out, also yearning for a taste of carefree joy, as the aunties snatch, but then retract, tugging instead on her Yiayia's[2] sleeve.

"They've taken more bonbons than they should…"

Yiayia Eleni shoots a look that silences her complaint.

"Oussou kori mou,[3] do you want the whole village to hear?!" she shushes, pressing a finger to her parched lips. "Don't worry your little head about it. It's a tradition, even if they take more than their share." She softens. "They all hope their daughters find happiness like you. Sweet dreams come from sugared almonds under your pillow, remember."

Yiota scoffs. *They're very welcome to mine!*

The room pulses with forced merriment, wide grins stretching across loud voices. *If only Baba were here, none of this would be happening. No one cares about what I want*, the bitter truth hanging at the edge of her tongue.

Andriannou raises an eyebrow. "Sit still, Yiota," she orders. "Hold your head high. Today is about happiness." She steps closer, her grip tightening on her daughter's waist.

"Straighten your back, prokomeni,"[4] she says icily. "Make your mother proud."

The sapphire pouffe feels like a stage, thrusting Yiota into an unwanted spotlight. A sea of black headscarves sways before her, each aunt a judge. Their proverbs crash against her

"Eshis korin is tin sousan, ta proitzia is tin sentoukan."

(If you have a daughter in her cradle, you should have already prepared her dowry in a chest.)

A chalky taste coats her mouth and dread coils in her stomach. *Dowry. Marriage.* A lifetime of servitude packaged as fate.

She recognises the faces, a blend of blood and obligation, that form the village's social court. Aunties circle the marital bed, bickering over who will be the first to bless it. Others occupy wicker chairs, their eyes wide with curiosity, their lips moving in hushed gossip. Delicate coffee cups, held high with exaggerated poise, tremble in their hands. Laughter lines crinkle around their eyes as they recount their own wedding nights, offering dubious wisdom on wifely duties – secrets shared only among the initiated.

"A little pinch! You won't even blink," an auntie squeals, overly optimistic.

"Lies, Skevou!" another retorts, wiping coffee from her lip. "It hurts, especially unprepared. She needs to know!"

Adriannou scolds, placing a hand on her daughter's shoulder. "You're scaring her, Maria. Don't worry, Yiotoulla[5] mou, you'll be fine."

Pantelou, the eldest, commands quietness with a raised hand. "Listen, Kori. Be strong, okay? Pretend you love it. Your charm and... well, pleasing him are your only weapons. Understand?"

Yiota's aunts share their wisdom like a Sophoclean chorus, turning the girl into a petrified statue. Her ears strain to decipher their patchwork of marriage, veiled anatomy stitched into convention.

Yiayia Eleni murmurs and reaches out with shaky hands. "On your wedding night, child," she clears her throat, "after the... business... your husband will expect proof."

A tiny vial, glinting like a ruby eye, appears in her palm. Its crimson contents pulse with sinister promise.

"If nature doesn't cooperate," her eyes plead, "use this. We can't have his family think less of us... and besides, poor rooster died for a good cause, didn't he?!"

Yiota's hand closes around the vial, careful not to shatter the hopes of generations.

Andriannou's eyes quickly pick up on her daughter's distress. "Yiavrin[6] mou, this is what it means to be a woman."

Yiota nods, horrified. *Was the rooster from last night's dinner the same one in this vial?*

The aunties drone on, oblivious to the secrets etched on the girl's young body, a conquest from nights before. Claimed, owned, mirroring the colonised land of her birth. Secrets fester in this room, echoing with generations of unspoken pain, a tight-lipped theatre where women play their roles behind a facade of acceptance.

Yiota's attention drifts to the photograph of Demetraki sitting on her dressing table, a reminder of the man her family has chosen for her. He is a Cypriot from Zaïre, a place as mysterious and vast as the Congo River that swallows all others. At 28, Demetraki is their financial saviour and Yiota, only 14, is the price. His handsome face, framed by dark skin and jet-black hair styled in a quiff, dominates the room. Solid eyebrows arching above hooded eyes, set close together, define his sharp features, lending him an intense, almost brooding air. He moved in weeks before the wedding, setting tongues wagging among the village aunties.

A hot blush creeps up her neck. *Oh God! Yiayia must know.* Relief flickers. *At least after we're married, he won't sneak into my room.* Duty pulls the girl towards Demetraki's confident exterior, but to him, she's a mere clay pot with handles, easily moulded and grasped.

"Kori mou," whispers Yiayia Eleni, "where has your mind taken you this time?" Yiota turns away, her bottom lip sticking out.

"No thought is worth that gloomy face. Watch out, that frown will stick if the wind picks up."

"That's not true," she giggles nervously. "I don't want this. I want other things in my life."

"But you like him, don't you?" Eleni asks, noticing Yiota's cheeks flush red. "Eh...We're not allowed to dream of different lives. We're here to serve our family. Look on the bright side. You like him, so it makes it easier. I had to learn to like your grandfather. You're lucky."

Simple answers to complex feelings only make Yiota's frustration grow.

The aunties dress the girl in a white lace gown with beaded embroidery, pulling the veil over her face. "This will protect you from the evil eye," one says. Yiota's throat clenches as the time to be paraded through the village nears.

"Mamma..." she pleads to Andriannou.

"Panayiota!" her mother counters, using her full name. "Your marriage to this man is necessary. You must become the bridge your family can walk over to survive." She turns and walks away, cutting off any potential argument. Behind the veil, Yiota's eyes well up, her brow furrowing in tacit protest.

Decades later, my Yiayia, Panayiota, frequently reflected on her mother's words and recounted her experiences in lengthy monologues that I had (no choice but) to memorise word-for-word. In the last stages of her Alzheimer's, all her memories – all of the faces, events, and places – merged and confabulated into one.

"On our way to Zaïre after the wedding, we stopped in Brussels to catch a connecting flight," she repeated. "Your Bappou, Demetraki, took me to a boutique. He was adamant I needed new clothes, even though Mamma had made me lovely dresses. 'Cypriot clothes aren't good enough for where we're going,' he said as if I should pass for one of those fancy British women who visited our village and looked down on us. He told me to pick out anything I wanted. The shop was full of hats, gowns and silk and it smelled like vanilla – a scent I'd never known. I was overwhelmed by all the choices. How could I enjoy such luxuries when my family back home had nothing? The shop women watched me curiously and whispered in French. I spotted a porcelain doll with golden hair and a blue dress on a shelf. I touched its embroidery and felt the soft velvet. It looked so real, sitting there alone. I wanted it for the company. I didn't care about the clothes. 'Demetraki...' I said, pointing to the doll, 'I just want that.'"

1   *Allamata* in the Greek Cypriot dialect is the wedding ritual of adornment and happens before the procession to church. It translates to 'change of clothes', which is symbolic of the rite of passage that marks this ceremony.
2   The Greek term *Yiayia* translates to 'Grandmother'.
3   *Kori mou* is a Greek-speaking Cypriot term of endearment used in dialect meaning 'my daughter'.
4   The Greek term *Prokomeni* translates to 'diligent and dutiful', and can be interpreted as 'cut from good cloth' or 'pre-cut to precise measurements'.
5   The diminutive *oulla* at the end of a name is used in the Greek-Cypriot speaking dialect as a form of affection.
6   The Greek term *Yavrin* comes from the Turkish *Yavrum*. It means 'my little one' and is used as a term of endearment.

Chris Fite-Wassilak

Extract from *Emmental and Immortality: Cheese, Cleanliness, Disgust and the Unhygienic Story of the Long 20th Century*

O n quiet days at the market as a cheesemonger – once we'd finished stacking hard cheeses, arranging delicate young soft cheeses and lining up cylinders of goat's cheeses, we would play customer bingo, ticking off a box when we served one of the types of customers that would reliably show up.

There was the Drunk Skier: "I had this amazing cheese when I was in the Savoie. They brought it out at the end of the meal. It was runny and very strong. I can't remember the name. Do you have it?" Any efforts to match the cheese inevitably failed, as nothing would compare to their searing, confused memory of the taste. They usually left with what was undoubtedly the exact cheese they had eaten in the Savoie, but still suspiciously certain that it wasn't the same.

Another was the Brie Detective: "Is that brie?" they'd ask, pointing at some random hard cheese and then walking away before they could get an answer.

The Cream Brigade would seek out only the double and triple cream cheeses that were stocked, smacking their lips loudly and moaning dramatically at the fairly straightforward, rich flavours such cheeses offered.

Hardman 3000 was out to impress: "What's the strongest cheese you've got?" he'd demand. Either no cheese was strong enough, his threshold was *so* high, or, the first cheese you gave him would make him clutch his mouth and slouch away in defeat.

Then there was It's Mouldy. It's Mouldy liked cheese, but insisted they knew when something was wrong. "That cheese is mouldy," they'd say, shaking their head as if it were a scam we were trying to pull. Blue cheese is the only cheese that's meant to be mouldy, It's

Mouldy would explain, nothing else. You could try to describe to them how tiny, sausage-like chains of *lactobacillus bacteria* are involved as milk starts to acidify on the way to being cheese. Or explain the process of mould-ripening, with spores of *penicillium camemberti* added to the warming milk as it curdled. Or where newly pressed cheeses would be placed in cool, damp environments to encourage 'cat's hair' mucor moulds, where the fungi digest parts of the cheese and help create the textures and flavours. Nothing would change their mind. Some It's Mouldys came back after buying cheeses, noticing that their cheese was "already going bad", seeing some tufts of mould on a rind and demanding refunds; most were simply enraged. "That cheese has gone off. I can see it."

Of course, cheese is always off. It's old milk, encouraged to rot in a range of manners. It's spoiled, even in its most highly processed forms. The question is, therefore, what sort of rot are you comfortable with?

In August 1903, London was invaded by six-foot cheese mites. For just over a minute, several times a day, dozens of the oversized bugs would scuttle around Leicester Square. Searching busily with bulging, squat, hairy bodies, some would turn in slow pirouettes, others churning along as if in rush-hour traffic, as they pushed and scrabbled among giant chunks of Stilton cheese. The newspapers filled with reports of the infamous insects, the British press calling them 'hideous', 'revolting', 'creepy', and – by far the media's favourite description – 'blood-curdling'.

These enlarged creatures were part of a new form of entertainment: *The Unseen World*, short films of microscopic life brought to you by the 'Urban Duncan Micro-Bioscope', among the first scientific films to be screened to a general audience. In the opening scene, a man sits at a small table arranging a snack of cheese and bread, settling in to read a news-paper with the aid of a magnifying glass, which, after a few moments, he casually trains on the cheese in front of him and gawps in surprise.

The film then cuts to close-ups of the bugs crawling and milling in spikey disarray. The magnifying glass set-up illustrated what the *Unseen World* films were offering: to take what might be sitting in front of you every day and view it large. The implication was, of course, that every piece of cheese is teeming with horrendous life.

Charles Urban, the film's producer and promoter, knew disgust was part of the appeal. His marketing described the film as full of 'great uncanny crabs, bristling with spiny hairs and legs'. The newspaper reviewers rose to the bait, describing the mites as 'awful creations of a disordered brain.' A common refrain in writeups on the film was swearing off cheese entirely, now that its bug-ridden makeup was revealed. 'I cannot imagine anyone enjoying a piece of Stilton after witnessing the first item of the entertainment', the reporter of *The Sketch* noted. At the same time, *The Morning Leader* promised, 'many a cheesemonger foresees failure.'

As the myth goes, in the wake of the popularity of the cheese mites film, the sales of home microscope sets (which often, at the time, would include sachets of cheese mites as part of a starter kit) spiked, cheese sales plummeted and desperate cheesemakers petitioned for the film to be suppressed.

The revelation of the incessant, ever-present crawling of the cheese mites fed into broader fears. There was a widening gap between what was known to be safe to eat and what was *actually* safe to eat, a gap that began to be filled with vivid and virulent imaginations. Cheese was already considered suspect simply because it was made from milk, at the time adulterated with anything from chalk, gypsum plaster, boric acid or hydrogen peroxide. Milk had also become a focus for potentially spreading disease, linked to fatal instances of scarlet fever, typhoid and diphtheria. By the time of the cheese mites film, cow's milk was also suspected of spreading tuberculosis, at that point a leading cause of death.

It evidently touched a nerve that here, in graphic detail, was proof that a solidly British cheese eaten by a solidly middle-class British gentleman was rife with insects. While eating mites isn't bad for you (and it still happens all the time), the image fuelled the confusion between safety, quality and visibility. If it looks hideous, then it must be bad for you, right?

Stories persist, even now in film history and Insta stories, of how the cheese mites segment was the UK's first film to be banned. In fact, *The Unseen World* proved so successful it ran at the Alhambra for nine months straight and then toured the country throughout the next year. The ban seems more likely a rumour stoked by Urban, turning controversy to his advantage. It still touches a nerve: people don't like knowing that little bugs might be on their cheese or already in their stomachs. Part of the cheese mites film's enduring relevance is that the reactions of shock, disgust and disavowal are pretty much the same today.

But the cheese mites' public and prominent appearance at the start of the 20th century, is revealing. New technologies were making the conjectural and the imagined visible. At the centre of the first publicly screened nature documentary series is cheese – used to convey the idea that what we eat and put inside us could now be understood in almost overwhelming detail.

The cheese mites film marks an inauguration of a modern hygienic imaginary: a perversely fascinated and paranoia-tinged relationship to the microbial world, enabled and amplified by new ways of seeing and distributing imagery. That same autumn of 1903, the Institute of Hygiene opened in London, part of a growing number of clubs, movements and societies set up to spread the new gospel of hygiene. The hygienic imagination soon springboarded beyond facts to imagine a delusional future for humans: spotless, germ-free and deathless.

As you walk down a supermarket fridge aisle or by a market cheese stall, consider the patchwork of cheeses an embodiment of where we are now. From pre-wrapped slices that hold a small enough percentage of dairy solids to only legally be called 'process cheese product', to pitted balls of mite-infested Mimolette – have a sniff and maybe a taste – these are remnants of the narrowing range of rot that we allow ourselves to glimpse in the world.

Mark Henstock

Extract from *Outrageous Fortune:*
15 True Stories About Lotteries

L eaving on a Jet Plane tops the US charts. The My Lai Massacre fills the newspapers. It's 1st December 1969, 8pm Eastern Standard Time. The words 'Special Report' cover the TV screen. "Because of the following broadcast," says the CBS announcer, "the usual programme won't be presented tonight."

Fade-in to a largish conference room. Under the glare of TV lights, a row of middle-aged men and women sit at a table with the Star-Spangled Banner behind. It's a committee.

Centre stage is a huge glass cylinder containing hundreds of blue plastic capsules the size of walnuts. To the right is a board, six feet across with rows of printed numbers from 1 to 366, each with an adjacent empty space.

A large, grey man – in his 70s, at a guess – approaches the microphone. It's Lt Gen Lewis B Hershey, speaking with an affected gravitas.

"Pursuant to the executive order, the Director of Selective Service is going to establish tonight a random selection of sequence for induction for 1970."

If you can't penetrate that cloud of euphemism, let me help. It means that on President Nixon's orders, they're about to randomly select those who'll be conscripted to fight and perhaps die in Vietnam, and those who'll instead be allowed to lead normal lives – to find jobs, to fall in love, to settle down. It's a conscription lottery. It's not the first and it won't be the last, but it is probably the most controversial.

General Hershey calls forward a Republican congressman who reaches down into the glass cylinder, picks up a capsule and hands it to a man by the display board. As he opens the capsule, the TV camera zooms in on his hands. They're shaking. He takes out a slip of paper and reads it aloud. *September 14th.* Someone repeats that, adding: *Zero zero one.* The slip of paper is stuck next to number one on the big board.

Of the men eligible for the draft, those born on 14th of September will be the first to go. They'll be drafted in January and be in Vietnam by June. The next number drawn is April 24th, the next is December 30th and then February 14th – Valentine's Day.

The TV coverage is interrupted by a commercial. It's a snow scene. To the tune of *Jingle Bells,* an animated Santa toboggans downhill on a giant electric shaver while a beaming voiceover glows with Christmas cheer.

Across the USA young men who've scarcely started shaving, drink beer they're forbidden to drink and watch TV with their buddies, waiting nervously for their birthdays to be drawn.

Years later, they still recall that night in detail, the friends they were with and those who went, but never came back. There was the anguish, panic, tears of those drawn early, and the unashamed smugness of those drawn late. There are stories of bizarre insensitivity – the man whose parents phoned him at work, telling him, as a 'joke' that his number was 3 (it was 335). Another man, who heard on the radio his number was 31, remembers the DJ adding, "Ha ha! You lose."

Most people say that one way or another, in their life's journey, this was the fateful fork in the road. People who got high numbers – above 200 – could breathe a sigh of relief and get on with the rest of their lives. Some became famous. Billy Crystal got 354 and decided to go into show business. Bill Clinton got 311 and abandoned his contingency plan – officer training – to go to Yale Law School. Donald Trump reportedly had a bone spur in his foot and was deferred, but the problem mysteriously disappeared without treatment after he drew number 356. He continued in his father's property company.

People at risk, with low numbers, started looking for a way out. They applied to the National Guard, which exempted them, or enlisted in the Navy or Air Force where the odds of survival were better. Some tried to fail the fitness test. One man starved himself until he was under the minimum weight.

Charles Brinton of Wilmington, Delaware, was born at 12.03am on the morning of 12 August 1948. His lottery number was 142, which meant Vietnam. But Mr Brinton had other plans. In court he argued his birth certificate was wrong, as it gave his time of birth in daylight saving time, when officially, it should have been in Eastern Standard Time, according to which he was born an hour earlier at 11.03 pm on 11 August – with a dead-cert-safe lottery number of 342. He won his case.

Draft resistance manuals told men how to pretend to be ill, or gay.

'Act like a man under tight control,' advised one manual. 'Deny you're [gay], deny it again very quickly, then stop, as if you're buttoning your lip...'

'All of my clients who faked it got their exemptions,' said a draft counsellor, 'but they drafted the one fellow who was really gay.'

The government raised the standard of proof required for exemption. It had an unexpected consequence. Gay men found themselves not merely 'admitting' their 'homosexuality', but actively asserting their gay identity.

Many registered as conscientious objectors and over 50,000 escaped to Canada. Half never came back.

But, within days of the lottery came news that it hadn't been random. Statisticians showed that the capsules hadn't been properly mixed. Born January to June and you'd probably escape; born July to December and you'd probably go to Vietnam. It was skewed. The later you were born in the year, the more chance you had of fighting and dying in Vietnam. The lottery had failed in its primary purpose: to be fairer than the system it replaced. Nixon's White House dismissed the statistical evidence as 'speculative' and nothing was done.

As I read the story at my computer, I feel a personal stake. I was born on 31st December – in the worst, unfairest, month. I check my lottery result. Low number. I'd have gone to Vietnam. Strangely compelled, I download the Vietnam War 'Fatal Casualty' data from a US government website. Five minutes of sifting and I'm looking at the lottery 'winners' who were killed – familiar-sounding names, some from cities but mainly from suburban or small-town America. I scroll down the cause-of-death column: *Small-Arms Fire, Grenade, Artillery, Self-Inflicted*. Several were born on 31st December. I pick one.

John W McLemore Jr, 24, from Fresno, California. He was killed in March 1971 near Khe Sanh, by small-arms fire in a night attack on his position. He'd been in Vietnam just a month. Online there are high school photos. Blond, with firm-jawed, right-stuff looks, John played for both football and baseball teams and was Student Body President. His high school still awards a John McLemore Trophy to a student who shares his qualities: loyalty, selflessness and steadfastness.

John's remains are in a Bakersfield cemetery. I find newspaper stories. His 23-year-old widow, Denise, turned his funeral into an anti-war protest and banned the Army from attending. No flag on the casket, just flowers. No gun salute, just peace songs. No flag presentation to the widow: *On behalf of a grateful nation.* None of that.

"Older people", Denise told UPI, "can't bring themselves to admit the United States could ever be wrong. If you truly love this country, you question it, you question what it does. That is patriotism."

Online, I find a photo of John's memorial, inscribed with the peace sign, and a dove with an olive branch. There but for the grace of God...

Rosie Kellett

The Lunch Lady from Upstairs

F ood is life. Food is love. Food is community.
I strongly believe these statements to be true, right down to the core of my being, to my very bones. I am, admittedly, a food writer and chef, so I am well placed to campaign for the love of food. However, I have always felt this way. This sentiment was most recently demonstrated to me on a cookbook shoot in late July 2024.

To give some context, the standard food photography shoot is often the scene of considerable food waste, anywhere between eight and 12 recipes are shot in a day, the food styling team source enough ingredients to make double of everything, in the event that something goes wrong and you need to start again. It's sometimes necessary to buy triple the berries you will use, because, for the picture, you will need a handful of the most perfect, juicy, fit to burst raspberries and there may only be a few worthy candidates in each punnet. You would think that everyone takes home the ingredients at the end of the day and this certainly happens on occasion. However, more often than not, the food has been touched, prodded, left out of the fridge and everyone is sick of the sight of it. So, come the end of the day, it gets binned, in the name of a speedy break down.

On top of this, there is the food styling to consider. In my experience, there are two schools of food styling. One is to employ every trick in the book to make the food look it's most appetising which, ironically, often makes it inedible. It's standard practice to use hairspray to make things shine, to paint a roast chicken the perfect shade of golden brown, to scoop instant mash, dyed with food colouring, to double for ice cream – it doesn't melt, stays the right colour and can sit there all day long. In fast food commercials, there will be a cocktail stick in every fry. The process of shooting a burger looks more like the inner workings of an operating table, with perfectly rippled lettuce tweezered into place, a seductive drip of ketchup applied with a piping bag, a glistening patty slick with nail varnish, a slice of cheese, melted to perfection with a hairdryer – this is food they want you to buy, but you would never want to eat. All of this trickery extends the shelf-life of the recipe, allowing for discussion, deliberation and time sitting under hot studio lights.

The alternative, and my preferred method, is one of capturing a recipe, seconds after plating, just as you would eat it, with no fakery, just perfectly delicious food, in natural light, atop carefully selected props and backgrounds. There will still be some light tweezering, twizzling the spaghetti with a fork into a perfect nest, sprinkling a few extra flakes of salt to glint on top of a cookie, a strategically placed basil leaf here, a drizzle of olive oil there – it doesn't take much to make a great plate of food photograph well. The main benefit of this system is that all the food can be eaten after the shot is taken, it can be distributed, circulated, become lunch for the crew and maybe dinner for their families. The downside is that timings are tight, you will have a matter of moments from plating to taking the shot, while everything is still steaming, gleaming and at its best. But, my god, is it worth it.

For my cookbook shoot, we had over 86 recipes to shoot over eight days. The schedule was tight. On any given day, we had to shoot 10+ recipes, all feeding six to eight people and making doubles of all the baked items, in case of a dropped cake, or a bad first slice. We were producing enough food to feed nearly 100 people, every day and, on average, there was a team of 10 in the building. As the author and producer, I was in charge of everything from managing the budget, ordering the ingredients, hiring all the crew, equipment, studio, supplies and making sure we stayed on schedule.

It was a daunting task but, far and away, my biggest concern was the food waste. I have been on far too many sets where the end of the day is a hurried frenzy of filling bin bags, an assistant tasked with disposing of them before the studio closes. I've worked luxury weddings in India where I've seen literal vats of curry poured down the drain while outside the gates, millions live in poverty. It is my greatest fear that I might contribute or be responsible for this kind of food waste, especially given the socio-economic climate, environmental collapse and cost of living crisis. So, in preparation, I looked into local charities where I could donate, encouraged friends in the area to come at the end of the day with a Tupperware and planned to knock on all the neighbouring flats to see if I could interest them in any of the days shoot loot. In the end, none of that was necessary.

We were shooting in a converted shoe factory in East London. The majority of the building was residential flats, with the ground floor home to recording studios. A few of my friends were, coincidentally, there as tenants. It all started, as most interesting conversations do, on a cigarette break. I had popped down to the carpark for my afternoon coffee and a cig. Sat next to me, on a rickety pub table, were a group of five boys (nearly men) sharing a makeshift picnic lunch of baguettes, cheese slices, ham and crisps – a beautiful scene. After chatting to my friend Hugo, a studio tenant, I learned they were the studio owners and building team, mid-way through converting a large industrial warehouse on the ground floor into yet more studios. I'd already fed Hugo lunch and the builder boys had clearly eaten, so I didn't do anything about it on the first day. Come day two, I had acquired the head builder boy's phone number and asked if they wanted lunch. The answer was a bemused, but unequivocal, "yes please".

In the days that followed, I became 'the lunch lady from upstairs'. Around midday I would stick my head out of the window and shout down to the boys, asking how many were in for lunch and if there were any new allergies. One sweet member of the team admitted that he had a nut allergy, but it "wasn't that big of a deal". I assured him it was possible to join in and avoid having to use his EpiPen. Each day I would take down a tray of freshly made food, whatever had been shot that morning, from cacio e pepe, to massaman curry, shrimp and scallion pancakes, loaves of cornbread, lemon drizzle and stack upon stack of cookies, blondies and biscuits. Upstairs, my team would all peak their heads out of the window and revel in watching the boys hungrily tuck into the food and demolish the lot in moments. There is nothing more gratifying to me than feeding people delicious food and seeing them enjoy and appreciate it.

While I was working my socks off day and night to deliver a cookbook, a real career goal for me, the highlight of my day was feeding the building boys downstairs and being known as the lunch lady from upstairs. Between feeding my team, friends and neighbours in the building, sending food back home to my housemates and fuelling the builder boys downstairs, we didn't waste a scrap of food. At the end of the day, I would open the door to a spotlessly clean tray and a stack of beers, by way of thanks. As the days wore on, we got to know each other over lunch and cigarettes. It became clear that the building they were refurbing might sit empty for a while and they asked if I might like to host a supper club as a one-off event there, with them providing the music and venue. What started as a food waste solution had become a soul-enriching exchange, leading to future collaborations and further solidifying my belief that food is the most powerful, universal language. It's one we all must speak; our lives depend on it.

Avril Millar

Extract from *Accidental Burns*

P art of the course requirement is to find summer work each year in your area of study, to get real-life experience. So, that June of 1971, the chemical engineers are in labs, the mechanicals in shipyards and machine rooms, the electricals in power stations, and the computing students – of which there are very few – are hunched over huge machines churning out dot matrix pictures of naked ladies with their newly acquired coding skills, thinking they're changing the world. Idiots. I know they're useless nerds and thank God I didn't take that degree.

One classmate is up in the Highlands on bridge repairs and another has disappeared to the Borders to work on a road build. In both cases, they had sweetly put me forward to join them, but I hadn't even been considered. The engineers lived and worked on site, in temporary accommodation with Portaloos and shared sleeping space. No room for girls. I would have to stay in Glasgow, live at home and get to work every day. And so, it was the Corporation for me. A sustained campaign of telephoning and door-stepping finally got me to the Clerk of Works, a man just sufficiently high up the food chain to give me a job and low enough to relish having some power to wield.

The Clerk of Works physically suits his Dickensian title. Skinny-fat, with spindly arms and legs and a football of a tummy stretching his worn and faded shirt, tucked precariously into shiny-kneed grey trousers which overhang his unpolished slip-on, down-at-heel shoes, he manages to look dirty without actually visibly being so. He sucks greedily on his cigarette, looking at me quizzically.

"Engineering you say?" He glances over his pot belly at my application held low in his hand, his eyes squinting to read. "You want to be a Civil Engineer?"

I nod.

"And you're at the Uni?"

Nod again.

"They let you in?" He lumbers back to his desk, stubs the fag out in the overspilling ashtray and gives me a long look, up and down, through his billowing exhale. I'm slender, tall for a girl, bobbed dark hair, mascara and lipstick, with tight blue jeans, short boots and a cropped knitted top. I realise, too late, that I should have dressed differently, for numerous reasons.

"Well," he sucks his teeth, brown, uneven and snaggly and, although I can't smell his breath, I know it will reek of halitosis. "It's not the sort of thing we do really."

"What's not the sort of thing? Take students for work experience?" I know this isn't the case.

"We don't pay."

"OK." I know everyone else is being paid, even if it's just the bare minimum, but there's no point fighting it. I need the placement, money or no money. When I do a bit of modelling for the leather shop, I get clothes to keep and sometimes the odd quid here or there. I can manage on no pay. I just need him to persuade himself he won't be a laughingstock if he takes me on.

"I'll do anything."

"Anything?" His straggly eyebrows lift in a leer.

"Work. I'll do any work." I pull my top down to cover the sliver of midriff he's now inspecting.

And so, the following Monday I turn up at the Corporation offices and am walked by the Clerk of Works down to the yard where two gruff men look properly pissed off and nod to me to get in the back of a smelly, yellow van.

"Stuey, Ally," the Clerk nods vaguely towards the pair. "This is Avril. She's studying to be an engineer, apparently." It doesn't sound like a compliment. "Keep her busy for a few weeks lads."

They do.

The rat is big. Even bigger than the turd floating past my legs. The smell is noxious, thick and cloying, almost edible and, although I know it would be better to breathe through my mouth rather than my nose, I can't bring myself to do it. The foul impact of the stench assaults me and causes me to reel back, retching. A firm hand immediately presses against my back, pushing me upright and propelling me forwards. The walls are dripping with damp but, disgusting as the space is, the light streaming down from the open manhole illuminates the brickwork roof which, even through the horror, I can't help but notice. Between heaving gulps of effluent-tainted air, my dad's voice pops up unexpectedly from my memory, joyfully pointing out railway arches supporting tracks laden with passengers and freight. "Amazing, isn't it?" He would be looking up in awe. "See that? Held together only by internal compression of brick on brick and a scrape of cement. Pressure alone, Avril." He would look at me every time, at every telling, "pressure alone creates strength," he'd say. But Dad is not here.

The voice attached to the hand pressed against my back urges me on, stifling Dad's voice.

"Get a move on. You'll get used to it in a wee while."

The light strapped to his helmet casts a beam which lights the direction in which he looks. But I have no light and no clue what to do or where to go. My thigh-high wellies, thrust into my hands by the larger of the two with a grunt before I was pushed down the manhole ladder and instructed to put on by a series of hand movements and nods rather than words, mercifully breach the surface of the flowing sewage. I look down constantly and ineffectually to check that my stupid, new, pale blue jeans are not getting wet, reluctant to put my hands down to feel, for fear of what they will touch and in terror of losing my balance. The other, skinnier man, unseen but heard, plops off the vertical, slimy, iron ladder into the flow of water and strides past me, causing mini tidal waves of effluent, tissues, dead creatures and rotting foliage. He's irredeemably cheerful, because he knows what has to be done and because he can torture me with my ignorance.

NON-FICTION

"Come on, hen, get a shift on. This'll no' do itself."

We trudge forward, both men certain in their steps and confident of their ability to stay upright. This particular section is new to them but also similar to those they had taken before on previous expeditions, so there is no hesitation, no uncertainty. When we arrive at a fork, the tunnel splitting into two and disappearing into the darkness, left and right, they both march to the left and shout to me trailing behind.

"You take that one, we'll catch you up in a bit."

It can't be more than thirty seconds before they burst out laughing, but in that time, I feel I might die down here. I look behind me but can no longer see the light from the manhole from which we've come, the sewer having curved without me even noticing. I can't hear the traffic above our heads and struggle to even remember that it had been a bright, sunny, cold morning when we had climbed down. Frozen to the spot but desperate not to show my fear, I step forward in the direction of the right tunnel.

"Oh, for fuck's sake Ally, stop pissing around with the lass."

Stuey swings his head in my direction and his headlamp casts Ally into a huge, foreboding shape, now striding towards me with great sloshing, stinking steps. I feel, rather than see, his arm reaching out for me and he grabs me in a firm hold around my shoulders.

"Well done, hen. We thought you'd have legged it by now." He clutches my left arm by the elbow and half lifts me, stepping forwards into the gloom. "Let's go and see what we find down here then."

And thus begins my first day as a civil engineer.

Helena Pickup

Extract from *Fatal Luxury*

L ouis XIV was, famously, a man of routine. Ceremonies, council meetings, walks, meals and hunting trips followed one another in orderly succession. 'With an almanac and a watch,' said the Duc de Saint-Simon, 'you could be three hundred leagues away and know exactly what he was doing.' But popular tradition records an occasion when the Sun King's schedule was unexpectedly interrupted – by a fish.

It happened at Marly, the private residence created by the King as a retreat from the crowds at Versailles. 'The King is going to build a house between Versailles and Saint-Germain at a place called Marly,' wrote a duchess in June 1679, 'they say it will be an earthly paradise.' As with the Garden of Eden, access to Marly was strictly limited. Uninvited guests, however eminent, were turned away at the gilded gates. Informed that an unexpected party of visitors including two dukes and the legitimate son of a former mistress had arrived, the King's response was, "Well, they can go away again!"

Admission had to be requested in person from the King with the words, 'Sire, Marly?' Men could come if their wives were invited, but not vice versa. 'It was a great favour to obtain permission to go to Marly,' said the Marquis de Sources, 'and few people dared to ask it.' The King himself edited the guest list. Sometimes he filled Marly to overflowing; sometimes excluded all but a favoured few. He might choose to honour a powerful noble family, or make an exception to welcome an untitled Parisian banker from whom he needed a loan. The fraught etiquette around Marly may appear trivial, but it underlined the central truth of Louis's reign, his life and the age in which he lived – the King held absolute power.

Those who secured the coveted invitation entered an enchanted land, protected by high walls, the haunt of marble gods and goddesses, rich with foliage against which slim white fountain jets rose and fell. No expense was spared to bring water to Marly for the pools, cascades and water features in which the King delighted. An aqueduct and a hydraulic pumping station, the Machine de Marly, were built to channel the waters of the Seine to the insatiable fountains of Marly and Versailles. The Versailles fountains could not run at full power all together. When Louis went for a walk, they had to be started and stopped individually by staff who used whistles to keep track of the King's progress. At Marly, however, Louis insisted that the fountains play all day long.

Marly was designed as a compound, not a monolithic chateau. A central pavilion, for the King and his family, was decorated with frescoes evoking Louis XIV's avatar, the sun god Apollo and Thetis, the marine goddess who welcomed him back under the sea at the end of the day. The fireplaces smoked, but the King refused to raise the chimneys as it would have ruined the symmetry of the roofline. On either side of the royal residence was a row of six guest pavilions. One sun, twelve planets.

The royal apartments were decorated according to the contemporary hierarchy of colour. Red, the most prestigious, was for the King; green, associated with love and femininity, for the Queen. As the Queen died before Marly was complete, it was the King's secret new wife, Madame de Maintenon, who played Thetis to his Apollo. The marriage could not be openly acknowledged: Maintenon came from an impoverished noble family, deep in the provinces, not royalty. Known affectionately as, 'Your Solidity,' by Louis, who appreciated her wisdom and serenity, she took on much of the responsibility of a queen without the title, the jewels or the crown.

The white-and-gold octagonal salon at the heart of the royal pavilion hosted masquerades, concerts and games of chance with valuable prizes. These tokens of royal largesse included money, jewellery and delicate trinkets such as porcelain vases. Oblivious to 'the poverty to which most of the kingdom was reduced,' as Sourches put it, the King's guests gambled for enormous sums through one day and into the next. Retreating to the smaller pavilions in the gardens, they found everything provided for them. Wood and candles, which they had to bring with them to other palaces, were complimentary here. There were refreshments: tea, coffee, hot chocolate, liqueurs. There were writing implements, toiletries, dressing-gowns, ewers and chamber pots in white-glazed earthenware decorated with a crowned M in blue.

The King organised endless amusements: sledging parties, hunting breakfasts, opera, puppet shows, fireworks. There was a swing boat, an outdoor chess table, even a primitive rollercoaster. Marly was somewhere between a casino, a theme park and a luxury hotel.

It was also a working palace. Louis took meetings and read dispatches, occasionally received dignitaries. Duty done, he turned to a favourite hobby, horticulture. Lawns, flowers, trees and topiary appeared and vanished at the royal whim. The King's sister-in-law, Liselotte von der Pfalz, Duchesse d'Orléans, once spent an hour and a half viewing the King's tulips. 'A Scottish milord came the day before yesterday especially to see them and said that one of them was worth 2,000 francs; he is a connoisseur of flowers and has travelled widely in order to see beautiful flowers: England, Holland, everywhere famed for flowers, but he says he has never seen any as rare and fine as those of Marly.' If the Scottish expert was right, the value of one tulip could have supported a labourer's family for more than six years.

In 1702 Louis introduced a new element: carp. Carp had been a staple in French fishponds since the Middle Ages, a resource for fast days when meat could not be eaten. The King valued them for their beauty. In their majestic, stately pace, their vivid colours, he saw himself reflected. He collected them, fishing them from the royal estates, accepting barrels of them as gifts from the courtiers, buying them from fishmongers. After a delivery the royal family would gather to watch the carp tumble into their pool and choose names for them: Dawn, Pearl, Topaz, Mille-Fleurs, Beauty, Chrysolite. Liselotte was fascinated by their rainbow colours: 'some like gold, others like silver, others crimson and blue, flecked with yellow, black and white, blue and white, golden brown and white, white and golden brown with red spots, with black spots, in other words all sorts to be wondered at.' The ornamental ponds, with their polychrome tiles, gilt-lead statues and enamelled flowers, were the perfect setting. Pastries were baked in the royal kitchens especially for the carp.

A satirical song sung by the Parisians, one of many such songs which were the memes of their day, records what happened next.

To Marly comes a courier
Who should be seen at once.
But the guard at the door
Says: Get out of here!
The favourite carp is dead
No-one gets in today.

The 1793 source which records this song provides a few more details. Failing to see his favourite fish, named La Dorée (which translates as, 'The Gilded One', but also sounds like L'Adorée: 'The Adored'), the King ordered the pool drained. The golden fish was found – but not alive. Devastated, Louis retreated to his crimson-hung apartment for the rest of the day. The doors were opened to no-one, not even a ministerial courier.

The King's grief, sufficient to distract him from his punctilious attention to business, might suggest that this was a rare occurrence. Far from it. 'The carp are like me,' said Madame de Maintenon, 'they are regretting their native mud.' Carp thrive in muddy, stagnant water, eating weeds, worms and insects. They cannot digest gluten or yeast. In the crystalline waters of Marly, fed exclusively on baked goods, they died in great numbers. The King was vexed and distressed, but he never solved the problem. Accustomed from childhood to the heat and glare of the spotlight, always ready to sacrifice comfort for beauty, he could not understand that it was the life of luxury he'd given his carp which was killing them.

Poetry

Sara Aghlani

resist

protest is in the pallor of cheek.
the blood that boiled
centuries ago
finds itself on the crease of brow,
the air that leaves a shriek of
brass stained plumage
waving across skies, an SOS:
trailing its history of fight
through to a wrist chained to
crows of iron.
they cawed,

free, free

        an eternity.

Sonya Massey

Another newsgrab, another bodycam
where a white man with a badge
waves a gun in the face of
the black person he thinks won't tell anyone,

                                    the story's the same but
                            the door number's changed.

She's sorry for being so black.

That it makes the hairs stand on end at the back
of a head that knows no ill;
but she's taken her meds, and then
                        she's sorry again,

her sorry lacks the colour
lauded the white man with a badge
who renders her emancipation the new Jim Crow:
self-inflicted fabrication – resurrect Sandra Bland,
so that they might kill her again,
watch the blood spill on the boil:
no one ever found culpable.

The water spilled before
the hamburgers cooled, before
the corner could be turned –
before we could know

Sonya Massey
Breonna Taylor
Atatiana Jefferson

The list goes on, and yet
in the name of Jesus,
the cotton is bloodstained again.

Now
the bodycam
turns around,

                    finds the caretaker at the Overlook Hotel:
                    a snow-faced ghost dressed in all blue,
                    maroon bourbon spilled over,

                              the man
                              on the cam
                    dances over a ballroom of graves,

                              the man
                              on the cam
                              waves,

                    the rest of us all stood still
                              timeless,
                    watching you

Afghan Girl

You sent your infantryman
poking a pistol for a camera
at a face that was mine.

Threw a veil over,
thrashed beneath, but

You vanquished the tents
and stole it anyway.
Drank the cool sherbet,
desert breeze and smoke surround your camouflage
erasing geometrics on the blackboard
long after you were gone.

Hard years were to come.
You would broadcast a sorry sight
at Nasir Bagh Camp,
the school we wrote our freedom into, where
the fiercest Afghan girl
told you *no*
with a storm in the eyes, but
was met at gunpoint,
the shutter's symphony a procured silence.

If you'd cared to learn our names,
you'd know we were better off
before you came.
Your picture made a farce of history –
ours.

Eight, ten – you say twelve so
I guess it doesn't matter
that I was a child, that
I was the world's
before I was mine.

The harshest life was yet to come.
but you were never very interested
in how we would survive.

You were never very interested to learn a thing
across borders,
about how we are Pashtun.

We are Pashtun

Rachael Li Ming Chong

You Call It Your Secret Garden

Little landing strip in front
of the cobbled wall, behind
the quarry site fence,
vegetables take-off casually.

Studded star of courgette flower.
Bean shoots and their tendril
curls around scaffold poles: the tender
fleshing of bamboo skeleton.

And in the corner, joyful bursts
of shark fin melon. Jade green
rind with mottled blush,
water-coloured then rain-washed.

You slice thick wedges with
your cleaver, it softens in *ikan bilis* broth,
disintegrates to a debris
of butter seeds and thread-plump pulp,

our source of perennial warmth
in communal dips of porcelain spoon.

Your master stock is a galaxy
rarely stirred. Mulled in ours, we struggle
to define its flavour – white radish and bone
float up to surface, it prefers to emulsify under.

We've caught glimpses of its composition
in your margin scribble: fermented
mustard greens, blood of beheaded
chicken, reclaimed crusts of *kaya* toast

scavenged from the floor
of next door's *kopitiam.*

Each element you've found pairings
to balance raw taste back
into palatable water, an expert
in alchemy on the translucence of soups.

Still – your stock eddies, continues
to thicken. Is it the other secret garden?

We see her wandering around the conifer trees,
smoothing back the earth
over each footprint, slipping behind
the shed holding the freezer chest.

You follow her there.
Her red purse urgent and full
of seeds, she spills them
into your outstretched palms.

We hear the echoing whispers
when the soup-fat pips burst
under our teeth, with each slurped
strand of shark fin melon.

I have smuggled these across oceans
and your soil is full of stones.

Winner of the Gold Prize for Poetry, Creative Future Writers Award 2023.

Learning to Succeed

How could it be – the corridor lining
your classroom, the green wire gate,
the store selling boiler parts – should slip
from the default architecture of your sleep?

You sift through scrolls of blueprints only to find
blocky accented lines, bricks and mortar
like molars overcrowding, your rib gaps widening
to expose a window of vital organ.

Your feet no longer fit your footprints, instead
practise how to redistribute the weight
into each stride, draw a map for all the places
you can stockpile steady pockets of breath.

Chicken bone.   Bus stop.
               Pothole.   Leaf.
The wind crossing your cheeks
will speed up further east.

Ask your seconds to sunbathe.
The pencils in your drawer are ready
to shed their cedar, the post-it notes dream
of their moment, heroic, to prevent milk-less tea.

The traffic lights entertain themselves along the A40,
and next to the acorns, sisters
will plant piano keys, extrapolate
where the tarmac might meet your feet.

So whatever the order of your forward:
back, forth, sideways – pause – forth, back,
for you, a cascade of broken chords
in each translated step.

Previously published by The Poetry Archive, a winner of the Wordview 2021 Collection.

Capillary Motion

My ancestors peeped over a pyramid of freckled pears,
through smoke ribbons of agarwood to witness
my graduation to words with more permanence.

No more pencil – a fountain pen, gifted from the family shop;
they *gānbēied* raucously at the promise tint in its trail,
Roman letters scrawled over borders Ah Tai Kong never

crossed. It came with a bottle of Quink, souped up with sweat
wrung from Po Po's neck towel and sirens circled
along the glass rim. They shook it wildly to infuriate the ink.

It fermented tartly in its cartridge and surged out
across paper lines, brittle-boned *hanzi* skittling
in its wake: *won't, can't, shouldn't, couldn't; pierce, piece,*

priest, belief; knock, knee, knowledge, knife;
a continuous line of cursive trans-continental ghosts
would tug upon, nodding as it held its place.

In science class I unscrewed the bottom shell to marvel
at its reservoir glow in front of the fluorescent fixtures.
I learned how to lemon-soak my words without applying heat.

The split of the nib - it grew tired, warped ink
to a manuscript of blots increasingly only I could decipher.
See now my hands, they linger. Waiting,

for the gasp before the mark, the flow of liquid into narrow spaces.

Previously published in Where We Find Ourselves, *Arachne Press (2021).*

Timothy Fox

john walked out into the tall grass with all of us watching

someone whispered *he's gonna turn his head into a jar full of fireflies*

and damned if he didn't do it

and then he reached right up and unscrewed the lid
and those fireflies went blinking into the night sky
where unblinking they stayed

Previously published in Levee Magazine.

daddy gone

stepped up out of the weeds
holding a rabbit by its ears

we called him daddy gone on account
his daddy gone and never come back

he said *watch this*
and pinched the limp rabbit's fur
tearing it clean
and the pink flesh fell out all in one piece

we asked how he learned to do that

daddy gone flashed his pocketknife
and set to cleaning the carcass right there
saying *some nights i'm an owl*

Previously published in Gasher Press.

on the bayou a boy

smoking cigarettes asks me
are you a queer

he takes off his shirt revealing his pale chest
the first time i've seen what they call a farmer's tan
and i want to press my cheek flat against his pale stomach

no i say

he smiles and says *oh i thought you was*
as he drops his pants and stands there naked
staring at me out in the open like that
where we could both be caught

Previously published in Funicular Magazine.

nobody remembers the birdman

granny says he lived two doors down where the empty lot is

be quiet says the nurse *stop that fuss*
but granny points a crooked finger toward the window

he's out there carrying his house on his back
feathers falling from beneath his coat

Previously published in New Writing Scotland.

Yanita Georgieva

Posh Salad

Since it's just us, we can look at this egg and call it a baby. One year
my body was serving a purpose (thick octopus costume) then another
(sea-slicked revenge suit) now I just Google hip pain a lot. I don't know
how I'd care for a tadpole, but that feels important. What would I do
with an electric blue jellyfish, its wet jewelled tentacles splayed in my
palm? Everyone says you'll know what to do, like a slippery omen from
the ocean's mouth. Every minute with children feels like a test. What
if they think I don't get it? What if after all those piercing critiques of
my mother, I do everything wrong? Every salt cliff picking its skin is
an invitation to jump. Some nights I wake up thinking I've ruined my
life. It's always the same dream: two sweaty hands, on the wheel of a
car I can't drive.

On the Recommended Countryside Escape

We drove for miles on the weekends without seeing one tree.
Silence swelled in our laps until it dented the roof of the car, cracked open
the windows. On the side of the highway, mosquitoes picked at my face
and I didn't bat them away, didn't care what happened as long as it happened
to me. Have you ever, out of boredom, wished for pain? The locusts? The frogs
coming out of the river in droves? A little suffering is good for you,
my mother likes to say when the power goes out. Without it, we wouldn't know
light or relief. That summer, the ferries so gave in to the waves,
they had to chain down the tables, the bags, even the staff, lest they went
up in flight. I ran all the way to the pier just to swim in my dress.
The big blue howled its patient howl.

Confession

I didn't cry enough the night I found out.
Sat there in the dark

and put food in my mouth.
I kept showing up to his flat

even after they had cleared it of his stuff.
Did my job. Sold a flight to Dubai.

Watched two men dump his mattress
in the woods and said nothing. Didn't cry there,

not even in the nice lady's office
when I asked how it happened and she answered

before I could stop her. I wish I'd held the word
in mid-air

for a moment or two.
It's selfish, a man writes in the Times, to say *I*

in a poem. To remember to take out the bins
in his absence.

In dreams, he wears a cream jumper
and acts unlike himself.

In Response to the Question

Have you ever watched a mother cat detach herself after a long and arduous birth? It's a flash on an eyelid. You blink and she's out. Sometimes you find kittens in the bushes, still pink from a previous life. When I think of a parent, I imagine a shoplifter, running fast with a carton of eggs. Sorry. Could we try that again? One time my mother was cruel to me. She snuck out for a drive and left me with two kids and a blood-hungry hound. What would you have done? Now, when I'm threatened with motherhood, I crack an egg in the pan. What was the question? Yes. I love her. I love every wide-eyed animal trying to live with the world. My mother is a shoplifter, plucking away at the truth. One time, I heard a kitten wailing on the highway and spoke to it until it crawled out of the bushes. Have you ever wrapped a dead thing in a towel, watched it lift its heavy head, and look at you like something holy? I felt like God, or a heart surgeon. My mother put it in a cardboard box and left it by a bin. Last night she told me she's getting a cat. One final thing. When you save a baby, it's relentless. Somehow it found its way back. Fleas and all. If she were here, she would say: that didn't happen. Sometimes I hold the phone to my mouth and try speaking. When I found out my mother was human, it rained for three days.

Ellen McAteer

Poems from *My Deep and Gorgeous Thirst*

Stormbringer

In your siblings' steps you find the sea,
between the fist of Ireland's edge
and Scotland's broken bones,
threatening any vessel sailed across.

To climb aboard will only capsize
your brother mast, your sister sail,
so you rain like it's kicking out the tap,
dripping along portholes, cold fingers

fitting cracks, soaking into decks,
unwelcome, chilling. Storm
and whirlpool at them,
hoping they will anchor.

A sad woman with clocks for eyes
watches for a break in her weather.

Emergency

When the metal folding cot eats my brother, and he screams as it
bites, I try to bewitch it open – *if I were magic, I would magic that* – I
forget the spell, and cry out for my mother, but she doesn't come.
When the white ambulance swallows him and me and, screaming
blue murder, vanishes like a pill down the throat of a tunnel, I believe
that our disappeared mother must be dead not to fly after it with
coat flapping black and feathered, the purple silk oiled like a seabird's
underwing.
When, finally, she walks into the hospital, clutching a red balloon,
smiling tight, my own throat restricts as I swallow my medicine,
paintings of rainbows lying to my face.

Urban Ravens

'I'm picking at the world like an angry scab.' – Jackie Leven

At the Castle on Paradise Street I'm
chasing grape with grain, picking
out which boi I want to flicker at.
The trick is to burn golden like the
flame of a lighter, leave the world
just warmer for your absence, like
lighting a cigarette, pass on an
amber glow that doesn't burn angry.
If they've been scorched, kiss the scab.

My Deep and Gorgeous Thirst

It started in the throat of my grandfather,
riding boxcars in the dustbowl thirties,
dreaming big rock candy mountains,
little streams of alcohol a-trickling.
Shipbuilding in Glasgow, wartime,
pubs that opened before dawn to
dull the drouth of the nightshift.

It sang from the throat of my grandmother
Irish come-all-ye's, craic with Rosie mór,
feywild tales, ghosts and playing cards,
her jealous husband spitting in the fire,
banshee sheep crying like children,
beaten children greetin' for
a wee bawbee she never had.

It mumbled from the smothered mouth
of my mother's mother, pilot's widow,
honeymoon crashed with the plane,
child actress become child bride to
an old man who could keep her.
He stopped her playing piano,
sent the kid away to school.

It rang through the hungry, damaged body
of my mother, whom they called 'Chai'
not child, in boarding school at three,
forbidden to sing, mouthing words,
carving her anger on the walls
till the nuns, in pity, fed her,
which taught her protest.

It prickled within my thin-skinned father,
whipped raw by the *don'ts* of a priest
who took a grim-mouthed pleasure
in describing sins that the bairn
could never have imagined.

Which taught him to wrap
himself in drink and song.
Tumbling down all those dry throats
into me, spirit sharpens the gimlet
in my burned mouth. I am under
the slow cold river looking up,
bloated like a trapped corpse,
drunk, and by drunk I mean
swallied, fou, drowned.

Shortlisted for the Bridport Prize and longlisted for the National Poetry Competition.

The pamphlet *My Deep and Gorgeous Thirst* was published by Verve in 2024.

Stage & Screen

Olga Braga

Extract from *Odessa Mama*

Odessa. Sound of aeroplanes from a nearby airport. Someone's kitchen. Broken photo frames barely hang on the wall, scattered old clothes and a poster of a glamorous brunette scrawled over with a large Stalinesque moustache. The poster doesn't match the rest of the interior as though someone has tried to put their mark on what appears to be an abandoned house. ALEXEI (18) and DMITRY (in his 50s) sit opposite each other at a table covered with remnants of an earlier meal, samogon, binoculars, a box of bullets and the guns they are dismantling to clean. Dmitry completes the task as though he's done it many times before, almost bored. Alexei watches eagerly, mirroring his every move.

Dmitry: I thought you served?

Alexei: I'm used to real guns not this/

Dmitry: Kalash?

Alexei: Yep.

Dmitry: Those are easier to put together, a monkey could do it. Nobody's gonna let you use them here.

Alexei: Why?

Dmitry:	Looks bad on camera. This ain't Afghanistan.
Alexei:	It was more fun back then?
Dmitry:	It's all the same.
Alexei:	Were you a sniper then too?

Dmitry quickly dismantles Alexei's gun and puts it together. He points the gun at Alexei.

Dmitry:	Pow!
Alexei:	Hey!

Dmitry points the gun at himself and shoots an empty.

Dmitry:	Relax squirt, it's unloaded.
Alexei:	Did you ever fire at people?

Dmitry laughs.

What's your number?

Dmitry:	*(Handing him the assembled gun)* Here.
Alexei:	How many did you do?
Dmitry:	*(Mockingly)* 'How many did I do, how many did I do, what's my number' *(slaps him on the head)*. What am I, your girlfriend?
Alexei:	I just wanted to know how it felt.
Dmitry:	What?
Alexei:	When you, you know powwwwwww!

Alexei holds his finger against his temple
and simulates shooting himself, drops dead.

Dmitry: Look Chuck Norris, we've established you don't
know how to use a gun, do you know what this is?

Dmitry holds up the binoculars. Alexei
grabs them and looks through them.

Alexei: They don't work.

Dmitry: You don't work!

Alexei: It's blurry.

Dmitry: Move the bit on the side.

Alexei: Wow. This is so sharp. I can see the blood vessels in
your eyes – check your blood pressure mate.

Dmitry: Are you slow or something?

Alexei: Huh?

Dmitry: I mean at school, did they tell you that you're... you
know, special/

Alexei: Thank you, Dmitry.

Dmitry: (*Spits on the ground*) Well ain't you a soldier's
wet-dream?

Alexei doesn't hear him, looks out of the
window with the binoculars.

Alexei: I never really went to school. That's why I joined. The
pay ain't bad and you get a gun. You can make a real
good career in this type of business. How about you,
why did you join?

Dmitry:	Why don't you tell me what you see outta that window? Maybe your eyesight is better than your technical skill.
Alexei:	I see trees I see sky I see grass I see a dog I see Seryoga's house I see Ivan's house I see/
Dmitry:	You should write a book, you're so good at describing things.
Alexei:	Sometimes I don't know if you're serious or joking. But yes, I *have* thought about writing a book, I even have a really good first sentence. Oh, look, there's Ivan, he's walking somewhere. He's carrying a bag with food, he's got a box in his other hand.
Dmitry:	A box?
Alexei:	Yep, a box.
Dmitry:	What kind of box? Can you read the writing? Is it bullets?
Alexei:	Nope.
Dmitry:	Gunpowder?
Alexei:	Nope.
Dmitry:	What is it?
Alexei:	Superior Blonde.
Dmitry:	What?
Alexei:	L'Oreal – Superior Blonde.
Dmitry:	L'Oreal – Superior Blonde?
Alexei:	And there's a picture of Claudia Schiffer on it.
Dmitry:	Christ, give me that.

Dmitry looks out of the window using the binoculars. Intense moment. Pause.

Dmitry: That's not Claudia Schiffer, that's Kate Moss! He's going to Seryoga's house.

He gives the binoculars back to Alexei.

Alexei: Seryoga's? You think Sash'ka is back yet? You know why they put him away?

Dmitry: Who, Sasha?

Alexei: Yeh, it's 'cause he was selling crack.

Dmitry: *(Laughs)* Is that what you think now, Sherlock?

Alexei: That's what they say, plus, you know, what else are you gonna do when there are no opportunities in life. Not everyone can get a job like us.

Dmitry: You watch one documentary on crack, you think everyone's doing it.

Alexei: That's 'cause everyone is.

Dmitry: Selling crack, here? Where's he gonna get it from?

Alexei: There's always a way.

Dmitry: Running drills without a clearance. That's what he got done for, his big plans.

Alexei: You reckon?

Dmitry: *(Smacks him)* I don't *reckon* Alexei, that's what IT IS!

Alexei: Christ, Dmitry I'm just making conversation here, trying to be friendly... there's no talking to ya!

Dmitry: Not on the subject of convicted felons, no.

Alexei:	Not on the subject of Claudia Schiffer either.
Dmitry:	It was KATE MOSS!... And all I'm saying is Sasha got put away for a real specific reason. When we're... when we're in a *situation* like/
Alexei:	Like a warrrr/
Dmitry:	There are always casualties, there's always someone who falls through the cracks. It's unavoidable if you want to reach the end objective.
Alexei:	What is the end objective?
Dmitry:	Who the fuck knows?

> *Subtle noises of a Ukrainian Cossack army from the 16th century. Alexei is startled, is it in his head or is it for real? Dmitry doesn't seem to hear anything. Fade...*

Maryam Garad

Extract from *The Last Days*

Scene One

> *Flenock Estate, Hammersmith.*
> *AHMED unlocks the door to his flat*
> *to find the cat by his door. He strokes her*
> *back and lets her inside. The hallway is*
> *filled with clutter and unopened mail.*
> *He heads to the bathroom to make*
> *Wudu. As the water reaches all the*
> *crevices of his arms, face and feet, he*
> *smiles.*
> *Beat.*
> *Ahmed moves out of the bathroom with*
> *his walking aid but struggles.*
> *As he enters the living room, he plays*
> *his voicemails to find several from his*
> *doctor. He skips most of them.*

Doctor: I'm calling to follow up on our appointment.
Rejecting any form of treatment will significantly
reduce your life expectancy and I urge you to
consider/

> *He deletes the message.*
> *Rearranges the praying mat towards*
> *Qiblah and starts to pray. He enters a*
> *Sujood position (head on the ground)*
> *and begins to weep, letting out a scream.*

LAYLA enters. She is in her bedroom, calling Ahmed on the phone. She paces up and down, nervously waiting for Ahmed's response.

Ahmed grabs his cane to get up and walks slowly to the telephone.

Ahmed:	Ya' Rub (Oh God) What do you want from me?
Layla:	Hi/
Ahmed:	I don't think the NHS pays you to fucking harass old people.
Layla:	Sorry, have I got the wrong number? I'm from Freida Publishing House, calling to speak to Ahmed regarding his manuscript.

Ahmed takes a seat on his one-person couch.

Ahmed:	Yes, this is him. What took you guys so long?
Layla:	So, I read your novel/
Ahmed:	OK.
Layla:	You sent a physical copy of the manuscript. Unfortunately, we only accept digital submissions.
Ahmed:	You picked up the phone and dialled my number to tell me that you are not accepting my submission. Doqon baad tahay (You are stupid). Don't waste my time, I am a very busy man/
Layla:	But I read it and loved it. I had a few questions.

Ahmed pauses and does not mutter a word.

Hey are you still on the line?

Ahmed:	Yes, I am.
Layla:	There's no ending. Why does it end with him walking home from the hospital? After all he went through, he just/
Ahmed:	What?
Layla:	Gave up.
Ahmed:	I haven't given up.

Layla's eyes widen.

Layla:	This is a memoir?

She looks heartbroken and tries to find the words to comfort him but stays silent.

Ahmed:	I have been writing this book for the past fifty years, it's a story about my people, my home.

Scene Two

Flenock Estate. Ahmed sits in the living room sipping his coffee and reading a newspaper, waiting for Layla to arrive. He looks at his watch and shakes his head.
Layla knocks on his door.

Ahmed:	It's open, come in.

Layla knocks on the door again.

It's open. Audibillahi min ashaitan ir-rajeem (Oh my Lord).

Layla: Your door was open, so I thought I'd let myself in.

                    Ahmed turns to Layla and shakes his head.
                    Layla nervously clears her throat.

                You must be Ahmed, I'm Layla. The editor from
                Freida Publishing House.

                    Ahmed looks up and down at Layla not
                    hiding his confusion.

Ahmed: You're late.

Layla: By like two mins.

Ahmed: And you look like a child.

Layla: I'm not.

Ahmed: Well, you still look like a child.

Layla: That's a bit rude/

Ahmed: How old are you?

Layla: You can't just ask a stranger how old they are.

Ahmed: You've read my memoir, no?

Layla: Yes.

Ahmed: So you know everything about me, personal details,
                that even some of my friends don't know. Is it not fair
                that I at least know your age?

Layla: OK... I'm 27 years old.

Ahmed: Very young to be a senior editor at one of the biggest
                publishing companies.

Layla:	Well, I've worked very hard.
Ahmed:	You should be very proud, are you proud of yourself?
Layla:	(*Laughs nervously*) I guess so...
Ahmed:	Do you not want any tea or coffee?
Layla:	I'm good.
Ahmed:	OK.
Layla:	Should we get started?
Ahmed:	Before we do, I want to know a bit more about you, if we are going to work together.
Layla:	(*Nervously*) Of course, what do you want to know?
Ahmed:	Are you from London?
Layla:	Born and raised.
Ahmed:	What's your ethnicity?
Layla:	I'm Syrian.
Ahmed:	هل تتحدث العربية (Do you speak Arabic)?
Layla:	نعم أفعل (Yes, I do). How did you learn Arabic?
Ahmed:	This is my rapid question game.

Layla chuckles.

Layla:	Apologies.
Ahmed:	Where did you go to university?
Layla:	Oxford University.
Ahmed:	Big brains. Who are your best friends?
Layla:	What has this got to do with/
Ahmed:	To trust you to work with me, I must know who you are, so please answer/

Layla:	I never made friends at uni.
Ahmed:	OK, tell me about your close friends.
Layla:	Don't really have any close friends, I'm friends with some of my colleagues.

Ahmed looks at her with sympathy.

Ahmed:	What about your family?
Layla:	Not really close with any of them.
Ahmed:	Cajiib (shocking) you might just be lonelier than me.
Layla:	OK, that was just rude.
Ahmed:	Apologies.
Layla:	Is the rapid question game over now.

Ahmed shrugs.

	I guess my first question would be, what made you decide on that ending?
Ahmed:	I wanted it to end in a mundane way, a way where the survivor meets his fate.
Layla:	If you don't mind me saying, it feels a bit incomplete. You took us on this journey spanning decades, you survived a shipwreck, lost your entire family, rebuilt a life in the UK all for you to just...
Ahmed:	But that's life, we can do the most incredible things, and our demise can be quite simple.

Esmé Hicks

Extract from *Peaches*

INT. KITCHEN – AFTERNOON – CONTINUOUS

NORA (31, never still, fears intimacy, resourceful) enters the kitchen, looking for the bin. She freezes. Her eyes widen and she stifles the urge to retch.

Shattered glass, empty tins and smashed crockery lie strewn across the black and white linoleum floor. The back door is open, its glass panel broken, the remaining glass in the frame is crusted with blood.

Any intact crockery, by the sink and on the worktops, sprouts mould. Half-eaten microwaveable meals spill out of the bin. The room stinks.

Nora edges into the room. She puts the empty wrappers on the worktop and picks up a sticky and muddy tin from the floor, which reads 'PEACHES'.

Careful where to put her feet, she plots a route to avoid the sticky mess. She retches.

An upturned wicker chair lies by the back door. She steps out into the garden –

EXT. GARDEN – AFTERNOON – CONTINUOUS

The setting sun scatters light over dying plants and brown patches of grass. Three metal dog-bowls glisten on the patio. Specks of slimy peach adorn the rims and tumble out onto the paving stones.

She looks back at the large window next to the backdoor. On the windowsill sits a plate of congealed milk, dead flies glued to the sticky surface.

INT. KITCHEN – DUSK – LATER

The darkening kitchen is now spotless. The once-mouldy crockery dries on the rack. The floor sparkles – no glass, no peaches, no mud. The wicker chair has been righted and sits beneath the window. A bulging bin bag leans against the door.

Nora stoops into the fridge – it contains two ready meals and a carton of milk.

She cautiously sniffs the milk and gags. She lobs it at the bin bag.

She stands back to admire her hard work. She turns the kitchen lights on.

Her eyes land on the broken back door. Nora kneels to inspect the bloodied and broken pane of glass.

The room plunges into darkness. She jumps, whips her head around to see—

ELINOR (82, sturdy Irish stock, stubborn, fiercely independent) by the light switch, barefoot, in a dressing gown.

ELINOR
Nora! Away from that door.

NORA
Jesus!

Nora stands up, not sure if she should hug her grandmother, her arms feel useless and awkward. Elinor grips the worktop to balance herself, unsteady on her feet after her fall.

ELINOR
You should be well away by now.

NORA
How are you feeling?

Elinor grunts a 'fine'.

NORA
Can we turn the light back on?

ELINOR
No!

Elinor grips tightly onto the worktop, a wave of weakness washing over her. Nora takes a step towards her.

NORA
Nan—

Nora reaches for Elinor's hand but Elinor pulls back—

ELINOR
You're good to bring me home but I need you to leave now.

Nora doesn't budge—

NORA
But Nan—

Elinor gives her a stern look.

NORA
Your arm, the back door – let me help—

She tries to usher Nora out but Nora resists.

ELINOR
Nora, it was good of you to come but you've your own life to live. I'm
fine.

*Elinor is losing patience. Nora looks into her grandmother's eyes, trying to read
her.*

NORA
I drove all this way—

ELINOR
I didn't ask you to.

NORA
I thought I'd stay the night—

ELINOR

Is it a hotel I'm running here?

Nora sighs, defeated. She picks up the bin bag as she heads out.

INT. HALLWAY – DUSK – MOMENTS LATER

Standing at the entrance, Elinor glances out at the darkening sky. On the wall by the door is a small holy font, next to it is a photo of Nora and her mother. This surprises and moves her.

ELINOR

Wait now.

Elinor dips a bony hand into the font and flicks holy water onto Nora's face. It hits her in the eye. She squints at her grandmother.

NORA

Thanks.

Was that a flicker of a smile Nora saw on her stern grandmother's face?

NORA

I'm sorry it took a trip to hospital for me to visit. I'll call you.

Elinor nods and sends her out the door with a little shove.

ELINOR

Goodbye for now.

The door slams shut.

EXT. FRONT GARDEN – DUSK – CONTINUOUS

Nora staggers out – surprised at the strength in her grandmother's push. Nora goes to put the bin bag in the bin when she sees that it's teeming with empty peach cans. She looks in the next bin – it's more of the same. She stares back at the house.

To see that Elinor is watching her from a crack in the curtains. Nora jumps and forces a smile. Elinor quickly draws the curtains shut - maybe she didn't see her?

EXT. FRONT GARDEN - NIGHT - LATER

Arms laden with groceries, with one hand Nora rummages in the plant pot by the front door for the spare key. She lets herself in.

INT. HALLWAY - NIGHT - CONTINUOUS

It's dark now inside. Nora slowly enters.

INT. KITCHEN - NIGHT - CONTINUOUS

Nora quietly peers in. The room is empty. She is about to turn the light on when—

> ELINOR (O.S.)
> I'm sorry. I'm sorry.

Nora freezes.

> ELINOR (O.S.)
> I know I'm late.

Elinor's voice is coming from the garden. Nora crouches and quietly puts the groceries down. Staying low, she peers over the top of the wicker chair to see—

Elinor on the patio, hunched over. Nora can't see her face. Two of the three dog-bowls are now filled with tinned peaches. Elinor pours peaches into the third bowl. Nora strains her eyes to see who Elinor is talking to.

Lydia Sabatini

Extract from *You Are What You Eat*

INT. SUPERMARKET – DAY

A shopping basket glides over a shiny white supermarket floor. An array of herbs and spices fall into the basket.

A giant sharp knife lands on top.

Then a cascade of boxes of paracetamol.

INT. KITCHEN – NIGHT

WOMAN squeezes olive oil onto her hands. Drops some salt flakes and rosemary into her palms.

A moan of hunger and desire as we see oil being rubbed over skin – so close we can't tell where on the body.

A hiss as the gas cooker sparks on.

A cutting board on the side. A slab of flesh slaps onto it.

An intake of breath and the flash of a knife.

Woman moans through gritted teeth as blood spills over the cutting board.

A small handful of bloody flesh falls into a hot oiled pan, which releases an angry sizzle, the sound of which carries over into:

INT. BEDROOM – NIGHT

Engulfed in the reddish light of the bedroom like the inside of a womb, we rove over the body like a landscape. Flashes of flesh, skin, hair, blood, at odd angles, like we've never seen before.

Over this the sounds of biting, cracking, scratching and moans of pleasure.

They build

And build

And build

Until:

INT. BEDROOM – DAY

A hand reaches for paracetamol and a glass of water.

Woman sits up in bed in a post-bliss, post-pain fug.

She burps heavily. Looks down lovingly at her naked body, now hairier.

For a moment we see scars all over her naked body. Chunks taken out of it. Wounds roughly sown up. Many of them look several months old.

She opens the curtains and hot summer sunlight spills into the room. Clearly some time has passed.

She pulls on a dressing gown.

Relaxed, she pads out of the bedroom into the:

INT. LIVING ROOM – DAY

The once white living room is now messy and grimy with red-brown spatters. All the plants are dead. She lies down on the sofa, which is covered in demands for unpaid bills.

Unfazed by the letters, she sticks a hand between her legs. It comes out covered in menstrual blood. She licks it with the sense of someone sipping their morning coffee.

EXT. PARK – DAY

Tinkling music. Woman sits on a park bench in the sun. No earbuds. Beatific, she stretches and caresses her body like it's the body of a lover.

Crisp crumbs land on her from behind. Music stops. Eyes open. She turns.

Sees a group of TEENAGERS. Some are filming her on their phones, others gawping and quaffing crisps like popcorn.

She rises. Canters away. Laughter follows her.

She breaks into a run.

A DOG assails her and licks at her wounds. She reaches into its mouth. Clenches her fist. It growls and bites down on her hand.

A DOG OWNER screams and sprints towards them.

She clenches harder and rips her bleeding hand out of its mouth, the dog's tongue grasped in her fist.

She races away.

INT. KITCHEN - DAY

She holds her bleeding hand over the counter and sucks at it without enjoyment. The tooth marks on her hand repulse her.

She yanks off her belt. Tourniquets it round the arm of her damaged hand. Grabs the sharpest kitchen knife.

A knock at the door.

INT. HALLWAY - DUSK

Woman answers the door holding the knife. Fierce.

The Dog Owner is about to speak, but is taken aback and falters. Steps back.

DOG OWNER
Y- You're insane! I'm calling the fucking police!

Woman shuts the door.

INT. KITCHEN - DUSK

The Woman saws off her bitten hand with the kitchen knife.

INT. BEDROOM – DUSK

Sitting on her bed in front of the mirror, she stuffs the sawn-off hand into her mouth.

Stops. Spits out a dog tooth. She puts the hand down. It tastes wrong. Rests her still-attached hand on it, forlorn.

The setting sun through the curtains casts a beam of red light right over her heart.

Her stomach rumbles loudly.

We hear heartbeat sounds.

Tears roll down her cheeks. She realises what she has to do. She licks the tears.

The heartbeats get louder and she sobs with the force of revelation.

INT. KITCHEN – NIGHT

Heartbeats continue to crescendo as a hand grasps the bloody kitchen knife.

INT. BEDROOM – NIGHT

The heartbangs mingle with the Woman's loud breaths as she sits on the side of the bed, clutching the knife. She slices a precise incision down the middle of her torso. Blood streams out.

The room blurs into a red darkness.

Kumyl Saied

Extract from *The Witch of Baghdad*

[NOTE: All dialogue in square brackets in English, all other dialogue in Arabic]

INT./EXT. HALF-DEMOLISHED HOUSE – DAY

UNCLE KHALID (50s) shields KHALIFA (8). Chunks of concrete explode around them, bullets pierce from every direction as they duck for cover.

Uncle Khalid steals a look out the window. The way out from this war-torn town is manned by men and women in uniform.

UNCLE KHALID
Ali—

He gives the boy a parcel, wrapped up in a worn woven cloth. The boy's small dirty fingers unwrap it to reveal the food inside, like a treasure. No more than a day's worth.

UNCLE KHALID (cont'd)
Protect this – and get back to your sister. Understand?

KHALIFA
What about Mum?

Uncle Khalid's eyes well up.

UNCLE KHALID
Majeed—

The boy is full of fraught hope. Uncle Khalid swallows whatever he was going to say.

UNCLE KHALID (cont'd)
Once we escape, we'll find her.

Uncle Khalid takes another cautious look at the destruction outside. He masks his fear well.

UNCLE KHALID (cont'd)
The soldiers can help us get out.

KHALIFA
Uncle, don't? —

UNCLE KHALID
I'll be back in a moment. Remember, our family is strong.
We are together and protected by the grace of God.

Khalifa gives his uncle an unknowing response.

KHALIFA (V.O.)
Are you with us? Are you really? If you are... protect my family.

Uncle Khalid braves the outside. We stay with Khalifa. He listens carefully by the crumbling wall.

Bullets and screams blend into collective horror as we remain blind to the carnage.

We hear a very short conversation in the distance - interrupted by a thunderous gunshot.

The boy sneaks a terrified look. His eyes search until he sees a cloud of red mist that thickens the air... behind this bloody haze is a brute caressing an oversized rifle. The boy's eyes track down...

By this soldier's leather boots are the lifeless feet of Khalifa's dead uncle. The boy is frozen.

A soldier catches a glimpse of movement, looks towards the boy, Khalifa ducks with lightning speed.

We can hear heavy boots march towards us.

Khalifa spots a hatch door; he crawls on his belly, through this obliterated abandoned home. He opens it and rushes inside.

INT. CELLAR – DAY – CONTINUOUS

Darkness. Each half-breath is loaded with fear.

SOLDIER #1 (O.S.)
[All clear.]

Heavy footsteps.

SOLDIER #2 (O.S.)
[Wait.]

They halt—

SOLDIER #2 (O.S.) (cont'd)
[Open it.]

The hatch door is ripped open, harsh daylight spills into the cellar.

VALLEY (40s) an imposing silhouette. She's a worn British soldier with conflicted eyes. Finger on the trigger...

She gets a clear view of the helpless boy clutching the food parcel.

A predator considers its prey.

VALLEY
[All clear.]

Valley shuts the hatch door.

INT./EXT. HALF-DEMOLISHED HOUSE – EVENING

Khalifa crawls out of the hole. The battle has stopped. The town that was violated by the sound of death, is now violated by the sound of grief.

EXT. WAR-TORN TOWN – EVENING – MOMENTS LATER

The boy walks the ruins. People tend to their wounded family and walk over the dead. He is all alone in a world without God, a world without reason, a world without hope.

Through the black smoke of a burning building Khalifa sees something—

A vision of a grim reaper in silhouette.

A hypnotic gallop beats towards us.

Hooves fire up a storm.

She emerges from the darkness drenched in black. Her hair blows in the wind like a fearsome warrior. This is NOOR (50s). Hollowed cheeks and screaming eyes.

An unresponsive soldier is flung over the back of her steed.

Khalifa trips over himself. He is struck with hope and a smile lights up his face.

> KHALIFA
> Mum?

Noor rips through the carnage, her black gown slaps the ferocious wind behind her... she takes no notice of the boy.

> KHALIFA (cont'd)
> Mum?!

She races past him like he doesn't exist. The boy follows her trail, but, through the devastation of war, Noor and her beast disappear into a rapturous cloud of smoke.

Author Biographies

A D Aaba Atach, a British-Iranian writer, is developing her book, *How Dare a Woman*, on Iranian women's silenced histories. Represented by Curtis Brown, she's honing her craft at Oxford and Stanford.

Sara Aghlani is a London based artist and poet. Her work is informed by living between cultures in Britain and she is currently working on her first poetry collection.

Noga Applebaum is a Jewish writer and lecturer, specialising in children's literature. Twice winner of the London Writers Short Story competition, she is writing a YA novel set in the Hasidic community.

Jess Barnfield is an alumnus of Faber Academy and was highly commended for the Bridport Prize First Novel Award in 2022. She is currently working on her first novel.

James Cornwell is a Cambridge literature graduate. He has worked in the centre of British Government, which has in no way informed his novel, a satirical whodunnit set in Chequers.

Carole Aubrée-Dumont's memoir, *Dumb*, was shortlisted in the Mslexia Memoir Competition 2020 and is the story of how the diagnosis of her son's speechlessness made her confront the silences in her French family.

Olga Braga is a playwright, screenwriter and stand-up comedian, who is currently on attachment with the National Theatre and has been commissioned twice by the Royal Shakespeare Company.

Rachael Li Ming Chong is a writer and teacher. She won a Creative Future Writers Award in 2023. Her debut pamphlet *The Red Strings Between* is forthcoming with Verve.

Louise Conniss is from Yorkshire and studied History at Newcastle University. She now lives in London and is writing a middle-grade series where malevolent fairies bring chaos to Victorian London.

Nicole Davis is a producer and writer from London. She is currently working on her first short story collection about hard-to-define relationships.

Yiota Demetriou's writing explores grief and diaspora and includes an artist's book, *To You*, her matrilinear memoir, *4757 Miles from Home* and *The Maos of Leonarisso*, a magical realism family saga.

W Y Dobson writes funny, adventure-brimming fiction for children, drawing on his Japanese heritage and previous life as a ninja. He has been shortlisted for The Bath Children's Novel Award.

Chris Fite-Wassilak is a writer, art critic and former cheesemonger, an editor at *ArtReview* and lecturer on the RCA's MA Writing, whose books include *Ha-Ha Crystal* and *The Artist in Time*.

Timothy Fox is originally from Texas. He has been selected for the Genesis Emerging Writers Programme 2024-25. His pamphlet *every house needs a ghost* will be published in 2025.

Maryam Garad is a playwright and screenwriter from London. Her debut play *Reparations* won the 2023 Tony Craze award and was shortlisted for the Mustapha Matura award.

Yanita Georgieva is a Bulgarian poet and journalist. Her debut pamphlet, *Small Undetectable Thefts*, received the Eric Gregory Prize. She is a former member of the Southbank New Poets Collective.

Mark Henstock was previously a charity fundraiser, managing award-winning campaigns around homelessness, disability and international aid/development. He writes non-fiction exploring the theme of luck.

Esmé Hicks is an award-winning writer/director. Alongside making short films, she's worked in production on feature films and co-produced *All My Friends Hate Me*. She's writing her first feature film.

Preeti Jha is an award-winning journalist in London. After training at the BBC, she spent a decade reporting from Asia. *The Myth Makers* is her first novel.

Monica Kam is a lawyer from Hong Kong, writing about unrest and change. She is interested in stories of her hometown and the shapes of its language.

Rosie Kellett is a food writer, chef and supper club host living and working in East London. Rosie authors a bestselling weekly Substack *The Late Plate* with 24k+ monthly subscribers.

David Lowe works in London at an in-house creative agency. He's a lover of all things monstrous and magical and is currently writing his first YA fantasy novel.

Lia Martin is a British-Romanian Londoner, who has been short-listed for prizes including the Bridport. She is working on her first novel, which explores the insidious effects of sexual trauma.

Ellen McAteer is a Thames-born Clyde-built poet and songwriter. Their poetry pamphlet *Honesty Mirror* (Red Squirrel Press) won the New Writer prize. Their first full collection is published by Verve.

Avril Millar is an engineer, serial entrepreneur and alumnus of the Curtis Brown Creative memoir course. She is writing a memoir about building a life worth living after adverse childhood experiences.

Marissa Mireles Hinds, shortlisted for the RSL Sky Arts Award and winner of the 2023 Bergstrom Studio Grant, is an artist exploring the Haitian Revolution through AGI, time travel and magic.

Margaret Morrison is a French to English translator with interests in genre fiction, bande dessinée and poetry. She also works in commercial/EU translation and lives between London and Cambridge.

Georgia Myers' short stories have been published and long-listed in competitions. Her second novel is about a badass bearded lady set in the gutters, fairs and theatres of Georgian London.

Helena Pickup, an art historian and former curator, is writing a non-fiction book on luxury, power and catastrophe from the building of Versailles to the sinking of the Titanic.

E J Robinson is a fiction writer working on a middle-grade folklore series beginning with *Swordfern* and a Victorian-set adult novel about a nun hunting Jack the Ripper.

Lydia Sabatini is a playwright and screenwriter, whose work has been shortlisted and longlisted for the Women's Prize for Playwriting. Her show *Consumed* ran at Camden People's Theatre, October 2024.

Kumyl Saied is a London based, British-Arab screenwriter working in film. He uses personal stories to explore existential horror and psychological drama.

Molly Pepper Steemson is from London. She writes about food, wine and adultery in long, short and critical forms.

Madeline Stephens did her English degree and an MA in Renaissance Literature at York. She has worked in campaigning and fundraising for charities. Her EWP project is her first novel.

Stacey Taylor is a writer from Cardiff. She has recently been involved in Literature Wales's Representing Wales scheme, as well as Penguin's WriteNow programme.

Helena Tebeau works in life sciences consulting and translates Polish literature in her free time. She explores the subversion of femininity and motherhood in modern day interpretations of fairytales.

Catherine Wilson Garry is a poet and writer based in Edinburgh. Her debut poetry pamphlet *Another Word for Home is Blackbird* was published in 2023 by Stewed Rhubarb Press.

Tian Yi lives in London and is working on a speculative short story collection about families and hauntings. *The Good Son* won the *Guardian*/4th Estate Short Story Prize 2023.

Acknowledgements

The London Library Emerging Writers Programme would not have been possible without a huge amount of support.

We would like to thank all the individuals and organisations who granted us the funds to carry out this Programme: Bloomsbury Publishing, The Bryan Guinness Charitable Trust, The Garrick Charitable Trust, John & Kiendl Gordon, Sir Max Hastings, Hawthornden Foundation, Gretchen and James Johnson, The Julio and Maria Marta Núñez Memorial Fund, Simon Lorne, David Lubin, Robert Macleod, O J Colman Charity Trust, Deborah Goodrich Royce, Sarah and Hank Slack, The International Friends of The London Library, Virago Press and a number of donors who wish to remain anonymous.

A huge thank you to the judges – Caroline Bird, Moira Buffini, Travis Elborough, Zoe Gilbert, Ayisha Malik, Emma Paterson and Chris Wellbelove – who brought their deep knowledge, thoughtful consideration, enthusiasm, inclusivity and, importantly, a sense of playfulness and humour, to the epic process of whittling many, many applications down to the 40 who made it onto the Programme. Thank you also to the brilliant readers who enabled that epic process and, between them, made their way through a record number (almost 1400) of applications.

Thank you to all the writers and industry folk who generously shared their expertise with the cohort in the writing development masterclasses and workshops, which took place over the course of the year: Caroline Bird, Lianne Dillsworth, Edward Docx, Travis Elborough, Eleanor Greene, Jane Feaver, Sara Langham, John O'Farrell, Scott Pack, Nii Ayikwei Parkes, Sarah Savitt, Alexis Zegerman and, from The London Library, Amanda Stebbings.

Thank you to all the staff of The London Library who worked so hard to make this Programme a success, in particular: the Fundraising Team, who have worked tirelessly to raise the money to keep the programme going year after year and from strength to strength; the Member Services Team, who make everyone feel so at home in the Library; the Membership Team for endless admin and logistics; the Communications Team who helped spread the word far and wide; the Building and Facilities Management Team who enabled the cohort to come together in the Library; Agnes Gill and Maia Berliner for administrative brilliance and general calm and Samia Djilli, Learning and Participation Manager, for supporting the entire running of the Programme. Thank you, also, to the Director of The London Library, Philip Marshall.

Thank you to Tom Conaghan and the team at Scratch Books for making this anthology into an actual and beautiful book, to Will Dady for typesetting excellence and endless patience and to Matt Bourne for all things design.

And, finally, thank you to the incredibly talented writers who made the fifth year of the Programme such a joy to facilitate, the 2023/2024 London Library Emerging Writers cohort: A D Aaba Atach, Sara Aghlani, Noga Applebaum, Jess Barnfield, James Cornwell, Carole Aubrée-Dumont, Olga Braga, Rachael Li Ming Chong, Louise Conniss, Nicole Davis, Yiota Demetriou, W Y Dobson, Chris Fite-Wassilak, Timothy Fox, Maryam Garad, Yanita Georgieva, Mark Henstock, Esmé Hicks, Preeti Jha, Monica Kam, Rosie Kellett, David Lowe, Lia Martin, Ellen McAteer, Avril Millar, Marissa Mireles Hinds, Margaret Morrison, Georgia Myers, Helena Pickup, E J Robinson, Lydia Sabatini, Kumyl Saied, Molly Pepper Steemson, Madeline Stephens, Stacey Taylor, Helena Tebeau, Catherine Wilson Garry and Tian Yi.

....

Claire Berliner is Head of Programmes at The London Library and oversees the Emerging Writers Programme. She is also a writer and editor.